D1245118

Kelley Wingate

Reading Comprehension and Skills

Second Grade

Credits
Content Editor: Angela Triplett
Copy Editor: Christine Schwab

Visit *carsondellosa.com* for correlations to Common Core, state, national, and Canadian provincial standards.

Carson-Dellosa Publishing, LLC
PO Box 35665
Greensboro, NC 27425 USA
carsondellosa.com

ISBN 978-1-4838-0493-4

03-085151151

Table of Contents

Introduction

Reading proficiency is as much a result of regular practice as anything. This book was developed to help students practice and master the basic skills necessary to become competent readers.

The skills covered within the activity pages of this book are necessary for successful reading comprehension. Many of the activities will build and reinforce vocabulary, the foundation of reading comprehension. These activities lead to practice with more advanced comprehension skills. Then, students begin to answer comprehension questions based on specific reading passages.

The intent of this book is to strengthen students' foundation in reading basics so that they can advance to more challenging reading work.

Common Core State Standards (CCSS) Alignment

This book supports standards-based instruction and is aligned to the CCSS. The standards are listed at the top of each page for easy reference. To help you meet instructional, remediation, and individualization goals, consult the Common Core State Standards alignment chart on page 4.

Leveled Reading Activities

Instructional levels in this book vary. Each area of the book offers multilevel reading activities so that learning can progress naturally. There are three levels, signified by one, two, or three dots at the bottom of the page:

- Level I: These activities will offer the most support.
- Level II: Some supportive measures are built in.
- Level III: Students will understand the concepts and be able to work independently.

All children learn at their own rate. Use your own judgment for introducing concepts to children when developmentally appropriate.

Hands-On Learning

Review is an important part of learning. It helps to ensure that skills are not only covered but internalized. The flash cards at the back of this book will offer endless opportunities for review. Use them for a basic vocabulary drill, or to play bingo or other fun games.

There is also a certificate template at the back of this book for use as students excel at daily assignments or when they finish a unit.

Common Core State Standards Alignment Chart

Common Core State Standards*		Practice Page(s)
Reading Standards for Literature		
Key Ideas and Details	2.RL.1–2.RL.3	5–16, 23–25
Craft and Structure	2.RL.4–2.RL.6	17–22
Integration of Knowledge and Ideas	2.RL.7	5–13, 23–28
Range of Reading and Level of Text Complexity	2.RL.10	5–18, 20–28, 65–76
Reading Standards for Informational Text		
Key Ideas and Details	2.RI.1–2.RI.3	29–46
Craft and Structure	2.RI.4–2.RI.6	44–46, 47–52
Integration of Knowledge and Ideas	2.RI.7–2.RI.9	53–58
Range of Reading and Level of Text Complexity	2.RI.10	29–46, 50–52, 56–58
Reading Standards: Foundational Skills		
Phonics and Word Recognition	2.RF.3	59–64
Fluency	2.RF.4	65–76
Writing Standards		
Text Types and Purposes	2.W.3	88, 91, 100
Language Standards		
Conventions of Standard English	2.L.1–2.L.2	77–88
Vocabulary Acquisition and Use	2.L.4–2.L.6	89–103

Reading Fiction

Read the story. Then, answer the questions.

Ethan liked to stop by Grandma's house after school. She would fix him a snack. One day, Grandma fell and broke her arm. The doctor said that she needed to rest. Grandma came to stay with Ethan and his mom until she felt better. Now, Ethan fixes Grandma a snack every afternoon.

1. What is a good title for this story?
   a. Helping Grandma
   b. Ethan's Snack
   c. Grandma's Doctor

2. What did Ethan like to do?

   _____

   _____

3. What happened to Grandma?

   _____

   _____

4. Where did Grandma stay while she was hurt?

   _____

   _____

Reading Fiction

Read the story. Then, answer the questions.

Our school has a new club. It meets every Tuesday after school. It is not a sports club. It is not a science club. It is a community club! The club members help our town by cleaning up litter. The members read to older people and visit sick neighbors. The mayor came to the first meeting. She is happy the club is helping others. I want to join the club so that I can be helpful.

1. What is a good title for this story?
   a. Cleaning Up Litter
   b. The Mayor's Letter
   c. The Community Club

2. What is another word for community?
   a. neighborhood
   b. sports
   c. science

3. What are three things the club members do?

   a. _____

   b. _____

   c. _____

4. Why does the writer want to join the club?

   _____

   _____

Reading Fiction

Read the story. Then, answer the questions.

Jared's mother teaches at his school. Every morning, Jared and his mom ride to school together. One morning, his mom had a cold and could not go to school. Jared called his friend Juan and asked for a ride. Juan lived down the street from Jared. Juan's uncle usually took Juan to school. Juan's uncle was sick too! Jared had an idea. He asked his mom to help him look up the school bus schedule on the Internet. Jared told Juan to meet him at the bus stop in five minutes. They rode to school together on the bus. They decided that riding the bus together was a great plan.

1. What is a good title for this story?
   a. Jared's Good Idea
   b. Get Well, Jared
   c. Jared and Juan Ride the Train

2. Which two people are sick in the story?

   a. _____

   b. _____

3. What was Jared's idea?

   _____

4. Where did Jared find the school bus schedule?

   _____

5. What might have happened if Jared and Juan got to the bus stop in ten minutes instead of five minutes?

   _____

   _____

Reading Fiction

Read the story. Then, answer the questions.

Heath is a fast runner. He always wins his class race. A new girl came to Heath's class. Her name was Marisa. She was the fastest runner at her old school. Heath wondered if she could run as fast as he could. They had a race after school. Heath and Marisa tied! Now, they are best friends.

1. What is a good title for this story?
   a. Marisa's Old School
   b. New Friends
   c. First Place

2. What did Heath wonder?

   _____

   _____

3. What did Heath and Marisa do?

   a. _____

   b. _____

4. What do Heath and Marisa have in common?

   _____

Reading Fiction

Read the story. Then, answer the questions.

   My grandpa was a firefighter for a long time. He helped save people from burning houses. Sometimes, he carried people down a ladder. Now, he has a new job. He does not go into burning buildings anymore. Grandpa visits schools to share knowledge about fire safety. He shows students the burn marks on his old jacket. He tells everyone how to stay safe. My grandpa is a hero.

1. What is a good title for this story?
   a. Fire Safety
   b. Grandpa's New Job
   c. An Old Jacket

2. What did Grandpa do at his old job?

   _____

3. Why does Grandpa visit schools?

   _____

4. What are two things Grandpa does at the schools he visits?

   a. _____

   b. _____

Reading Fiction

Read the story. Then, answer the questions.

    Vanessa's brother Luke is in the army. He visits countries that are far away. He helps people who need food or doctors. One day, Luke surprised Vanessa. She did not know he was home for a break. He came to Vanessa's school wearing his uniform. She was happy to see him standing in the doorway of the lunchroom. Everyone said that she was a lucky girl. Vanessa was proud of her brother.

1. What is a good title for this story?
   a. Army Life
   b. Vanessa's Special Treat
   c. Luke's Uniform

2. What are two things that Luke does in the army?

   a. _____

   b. _____

3. Why was Vanessa surprised?

   _____

4. What word means the same as *uniform*?
   a. shoes
   b. army
   c. outfit

5. Why did everyone say that Vanessa was a lucky girl?

   _____

   _____

Reading Fiction

Read the story. Then, answer the questions.

Kassie wanted a new puppy. Her mom said that she could get a small one. Kassie picked out a tiny gray puppy named Ruff. Ruff liked to eat. He was always hungry. He got bigger and bigger until he was almost as tall as Kassie. Kassie said, "I thought we got a small dog!" Mom smiled and said, "You will have to grow bigger to take care of him!"

1. What is a good title for this story?
   a. Kassie's Tiny Puppy
   b. Ruff Liked to Eat
   c. A Big Surprise

2. What kind of dog did Mom want Kassie to get?

   _____

3. What happened to Ruff?

   _____

   _____

4. What did Mom tell Kassie she would need to do at the end of the story?

   _____

   _____

Reading Fiction

Read the story. Then, answer the questions.

   I have a funny cat named Sam. He imagines that he is a dog! He likes to run after balls that jingle. He brings them back when I throw them. He chases his tail. He even growls at the mailman! Sam's best friend is my little brother, Robert. He follows Robert around the house and sleeps on his bed. Robert wants to teach Sam to walk on a leash. We are sure he can learn!

1. What is a good title for this story?
   a. Cat or Dog?
   b. Robert's Best Friend
   c. The Mailman

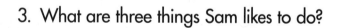

2. What does Sam imagine?

   _____

3. What are three things Sam likes to do?

   a. _____

   b. _____

   c. _____

4. What does Robert want to teach Sam to do?

   _____

5. What are some other things you can train a pet to do?

   _____

   _____

Reading Fiction

Read the story. Then, answer the questions.

Brian's little sister Kayce started school this year. They go to the same school. Brian introduced Kayce to his friends at school. His friends thought she was a pleasure to be around. Some of them had little sisters in kindergarten too. They introduced Kayce to their sisters. Kayce was happy to have new friends. She was also happy to have a brother like Brian. She hoped that she could introduce someone to a new friend!

1. What is a good title for this story?
   a. Kayce's Little Friend
   b. New Introductions
   c. Bothering Brian

2. What did Brian do to help Kayce?

   _____

   _____

3. How did Brian's friends feel about Kayce?

   _____

4. What did Brian and some of his friends have in common?

   _____

5. Why do you think Kayce would like to introduce someone to a new friend?

   _____

   _____

Reading Fiction

Read the poem. Then, answer the questions.

The Day Emily Sneezed

One very hot day, Emily the Elephant said, "I think I may sneeze."
    So, the grassland animals said, "Excuse us, if you please."
And ran, oh they did, for they were afraid
    Of what would happen when Emily's sneeze was made.
The giraffes ran for cover and hid behind leaves
    Of the thickest and tallest of all of the African trees.
The warthogs got up from feeding on their knees
    And frightfully asked, "Did Emily say she may sneeze?"
The falcon flew quickly as falcons can do.
    He remembered the last time Emily said, "Achoo!"
The earth had rumbled, and all of the trees shook
    Worse than any disaster you've read about in a book.
So, the animals all covered their ears and closed their eyes.
    But then, they got such a pleasant surprise . . .
Emily the Elephant did not let out a sneeze,
    But instead she laughed and made a cool breeze.
Now, all of the animals went back to their eating,
    And they were happy their land did not take a beating.

1. Where does the poem take place?
   a. in the rain forest   b. in the grasslands
   c. in the desert   d. in the swamp

2. How do you know the giraffes were afraid of Emily's sneeze?

_____

3. What had caused the earth to rumble?

_____

Reading Fiction

Read the story. Then, answer the questions.

Ma Lien

There once lived a poor Chinese boy name Ma Lien. He worked hard in the rice fields, dreaming of the one day he would become a painter. But, Ma Lien did not even have a paintbrush. Instead, he used rocks to scratch on stones or drew pictures with his fingers in the wet sand.

One night as Ma Lien lay in bed, he dreamed that he had a special paintbrush. Whatever he painted with it came to life!

Ma Lien used his special brush to help people. He painted roosters for poor families in his village and toys for children.

A greedy king heard about the special paintbrush. He ordered Ma Lien to paint a mountain of gold for him. Ma Lien painted a gold mountain surrounded by a huge sea. The king ordered him to paint a ship so that the king could sail to the mountain. As the king and his men stepped on the ship, Ma Lien painted stormy clouds that sunk the king's ship.

Ma Lien woke up and went to the rice fields to work. Eventually, he did acquire a paintbrush. Though it wasn't a "special" paintbrush, what Ma Lien painted was special. He remembered the dream and always used his talent wisely.

1. Which of these does not describe Ma Lien?
   a. He lived in China.   b. He was selfish.
   c. He helped people.   d. He wanted to become a painter.

2. How were the king and Ma Lien different?

   _____

3. Who was the most important character in this story?

   _____

4. What did Ma Lien learn from his dream?

   _____

Reading Fiction

Read the story. Then, answer the questions.

Paul Bunyan: A Tall Tale

The story of Paul Bunyan begins long ago in the woodlands. When Paul was a baby, he was too big to fit in the house! As he got older, he was so big that his parents had to teach him not to step on houses or farm animals. Back then, people needed lots of trees to build their houses and the railroads. The men who cut down the trees were called loggers. Since Paul was so big, he could swing his ax a few times to cut down a whole forest. He became a great logger.

One winter, Paul was out walking in the snow and found a young blue ox the size of a small mountain. He named the ox Babe. They became close friends. Babe would carry the wood that Paul cut down. He would also take water to the loggers. Paul strapped a huge tub on Babe's back and filled it with water. Sometimes, some would spill out and land in one of Babe's huge hoofprints. That is why there are so many lakes in Minnesota!

Once, Babe tripped and the whole bucket of water spilled. It made the Mississippi River!

No one knows where Paul and Babe are today. Some people believe that they are in Alaska, still cutting down trees. No matter where they are, you can be sure they are leaving their mark!

1. How were Babe and Paul similar? _____

2. How does this story say the Mississippi River was made? _____

_____

3. Why did people need lots of trees?_____

_____

4. How was Paul's job different from Babe's? _____

_____

5. Why was Paul such a great logger? _____

Story Elements

Read the story. Then, answer the questions.

The Cat's Bell

There was once a group of mice who had decided to solve the problem of the cat chasing them. Young Mouse said, "Let's put a bell around the cat's neck. Then, we will always hear him coming." The other mice stood and clapped their hands. They put Young Mouse up on their shoulders because they thought it was such a good idea!

Then, Old Mouse stood and asked, "Which one of you will put the bell around the cat's neck?" The other mice looked at one another. They put Young Mouse down and began to think of a new idea.

1. Which picture shows the beginning of the story?   a   b   c

2. Which picture shows the middle of the story?   a   b   c

3. Which picture shows the end of the story?   a   b   c

4. Write four words that could be used to describe the mice.

   a. _____   b. _____

   c. _____   d. _____

Story Elements

Read the story. Then, answer the questions.

Muffy and the Garden

Ella and her mom worked in the garden. They planted flowers. They pulled out weeds. Muffy is Ella's dog. Muffy watched them work in the garden. It looked like fun to her. At lunch, Ella and her mom went inside to eat sandwiches and fruit. Muffy stayed outside. After lunch, Ella went back outside. The flowers were not in the garden. The dirt was a mess. "Muffy!" yelled Ella. "You were bad!"

1. Who are the characters?

   _____

   _____

   _____

2. Where does the story happen?

   _____

3. What time of day is it?

   _____

4. What is the problem?

   _____

   _____

5. Who do you think caused the problem?

   _____

Story Elements

We have learned about the characters, setting, problem, and plot of a story. They are called the story's **elements**. Now, let's put it all together!

Follow each step to plan your own story.

1. Plan two characters. Write their names and two words to describe each character.

Character #1 _____   Character #2 _____

   a. _____   a. _____

   b. _____   b. _____

2. Where will your story take place? Write about your setting.

_____

_____

3. What problem will your characters face?

_____

_____

4. How will they solve it?

_____

_____

Comparing Characters

> Stories with more than one important character can be fun to read because the characters are usually different from one another, just as the people you know are different from each other.

Read the story.

City Mouse, Country Mouse

Once upon a time, a city mouse went to visit her friend in the country. The country mouse had spent the day gathering grain and dried pieces of corn in order to greet her friend with a nice meal. The city mouse was surprised to find her poor friend living in a cold tree stump and eating such scraps. So, she invited the country mouse to visit her in the city. The country mouse agreed.

The country mouse could not believe her eyes when she arrived! Her city friend lived in a warm hole behind the fireplace of a large home. She was even more surprised to find all of the fine foods that were left behind after a party the night before. The country mouse wished that she could live in the city as well.

Suddenly, the family's cat ran in and chased the two mice away. He nearly caught the country mouse with his sharp claws. As the friends raced back to the mouse hole, the country mouse said, "I'm sorry, friend, but I would rather live a simple life eating corn and grain than live a fancy life in fear!" The country mouse went back home.

The two characters in this story are different from one another. Mark an X in each box to describe the correct mouse.

	City Mouse	Country Mouse
1. She feasted daily on fine foods.		
2. She would rather have a simple, safe life.		
3. She gathered grain and corn.		
4. She lived in a large house.		
5. She was surprised by all of the fine foods.		
6. She lived in a warm place.		

Comparing Characters

Read the story. Then, use the details from the story to evaluate the characters.

Last One In Is a Rotten Egg!

"Hurray! We get to swim at summer camp today," shouted Logan as he jumped in the back of the car.

"I don't really want to," answered his brother, Nate. Every summer it was the same. Logan would swim away and have fun while Nate sat on the steps of the pool watching.

The boys spotted their friends right away, and one of them shouted, "Last one in is a rotten egg!" Logan turned to Nate. He saw his brother's eyes fill with tears.

1. What do you think Logan should do? _____

_____

2. What do you think Nate should do? _____

_____

Logan called out, "I'm coming!" and jumped in. Nate sat down on the edge of the pool. He watched as the others jumped off the diving board and chased diving rings. Once, a ring landed by Nate, and Logan came after it. Nate stood up and threw the ring back in the water. "That gives me an idea," said Logan. "You can throw in the rings, and we will dive for them."

3. What do you think will happen next? _____

_____

The boys spent the rest of the afternoon chasing rings as Nate threw them. "Maybe someday, you can throw the rings for me," Nate told Logan as they were leaving the pool.

Comparing Characters

Read the story. Then, next to each face, write two different ways the story could end, one that is the right decision and one that is the wrong decision.

The Clay Necklace

Miss Jenkin's class spent all afternoon working on projects for Saturday's Native American fair. Lynette and Jeffrey were to make a clay necklace. "I will work on the beads, and you can make the clay sun that will hang in the middle," Lynette told Jeffrey. Lynette carefully shaped beads out of clay and strung them on a piece of yarn. Jeffrey quickly made a ball of clay and smashed it down flat. "I am done," he called and ran outside for recess.

The next day, Lynette was sick and could not come to the fair. Jeffrey's family looked for the necklace he had told them about. There it was. Jeffrey noticed something was different. The clay sun that hung from the middle of the necklace had been carefully carved and painted. It was beautiful!

"There you are, Jeffrey," said Miss Jenkins. "I wanted to tell you how great your work is on the clay sun! You must have spent a lot of time on it."

Right Decision: _____

_____

Wrong Decision: _____

_____

Right Decision: _____

_____

Wrong Decision: _____

_____

Sequencing

Read the story.

Picnic

My family decided to go on a picnic. I started baking cookies right away. Mom packed bread and meat for sandwiches. Then, Dad put everything in the car. We picked up Grandma.

Read the sentences. Write them in order as they happened in the story.

Mom packed meat and bread.
We picked up Grandma.
We decided to go on a picnic.
Dad packed the car.

1. _____

2. _____

3. _____

4. _____

Draw a line under the best ending for this story.

We all had a good time.

We went to the zoo.

Grandma brought cookies.

Sequencing

Read the story.

Planting a Garden

I help Grandpa plant his summer garden. First, we go to the store to buy seeds. We rake the soil. We dig holes and plant the seeds. Then, we cover the seeds with dirt. We water the seeds so that they will grow.

Read the sentences. Write them in order as they happened in the story.

We water the seeds.
We rake the soil.
We buy the seeds.
We cover the seeds with dirt.
We dig holes and plant the seeds.

1. _____

2. _____

3. _____

4. _____

5. _____

Draw a line under the best ending for this story.

Grandpa buys a lot of seeds.

Soon, we will have vegetables to eat!

We buy a new rake.

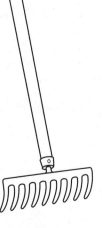

Sequencing

Read the story.

Painting My Bedroom

Mom said that I could paint my bedroom. She said that she would help me. We borrowed brushes and bought cans of paint. We changed into old clothes. We rubbed the walls with sandpaper. This made them smooth. We painted the walls green and the trim blue.

Read the sentences. Write them in order as they happened in the story.

We borrowed brushes.
We rubbed the walls with sandpaper.
We painted the walls and trim.
We changed into old clothes.
Mom said that I could paint my room.

1. _____

2. _____

3. _____

4. _____

5. _____

Draw a line under the best ending for this story.

My new room looks great.

I put on my old jeans.

My sister likes the color orange.

Character Analysis

> **Characters** are the people, animals, or animated objects that are found in a story. They seem to be brought to life by their actions, and they may even "grow up" or change as people do in real life.

Read the story.

A Real King

Larry the Lion had been king of the grasslands for a very long time, but the animals felt they needed a new king. Larry had become lazy, mean, and selfish. When Larry learned of this, he set the animals free and laughed to himself, "They will beg to have me back!" But, the animals did not beg to have Larry back, and so he moved away.

One lonely day, Larry found a mouse that was balancing on a branch in the river. He helped the mouse to the shore. Later, Larry found a baby zebra who was lost from his mother. Larry was kind and helped the little zebra find his home.

When the animals learned of Larry's kind acts, they asked him to become their king again. They needed a helpful and strong king, which Larry now seemed to be. Larry the Lion had become a real king!

Did you notice that Larry's character changed as the story continued? Complete the lists below by writing three words to describe Larry at the beginning of the story and three words to describe Larry at the end of the story.

King Larry at the Beginning

1. _____

2. _____

3. _____

King Larry at the End

1. _____

2. _____

3. _____

Character Analysis

Read the story. Then, circle the answers to the questions.

April's Dance Class

    April loves ballet class. She goes every Tuesday after school. Class lasts one hour. First, April and the other dancers stretch and warm up at the bar.

    Then, April exercises without the bar. She dances in the room with her arms and legs. She is graceful and strong. Dance class is hard work. Her teacher walks around and helps the dancers. He shows Nathan how to hold his head straight. He shows Becky how to relax her shoulders. He teaches them all how to pull in their stomachs.

    The next part of class is fun. April loves to jump and do pirouettes. They practice special steps and movements. They move with the music.

    April wants to be a ballerina. She works hard. She pays attention to her teacher. She never talks during class. She knows that being a dancer is hard, but April loves it.

1. What does April love to do?

   paint pictures   dance   ride her bike

2. Which words describe April?

   fast runner   hard worker   colorful

3. What do you think April is like?

   good listener   good writer   good babysitter

4. What would April say about ballet class?

   too long   really fun   very noisy

5. What does April want to be when she grows up?

   a clown   a dentist   a ballerina

Character Analysis

Read the story. Then, answer the questions.

Buddy the Cat

Buddy is an old cat, but he still loves to play and explore new things. Once, his curiosity got him into big trouble. Buddy almost died when he was a young cat.

One night after everyone was in bed, Buddy found a spool of thread on the floor. He played with the spool for a while. Then, he started to chew on the thread. Buddy tried to spit it out but couldn't. He kept eating the thread until finally it snapped. After a while, Buddy fell asleep. He didn't feel well in the morning. He lay around looking sad for several days. Finally, we took him to the vet.

The vet removed 26 inches (66 cm) of thread from Buddy's stomach. Afterward, Buddy was very sick and tired, but he was brave. He wanted to live. We visited him every day at the cat hospital. Buddy struggled to his feet to greet us. We knew he was happy to see us.

Buddy survived and is now an old cat. He is still brave and curious. He likes to chase other animals and explore anything that is new, even if it is dangerous. He has had so many close calls that we think he has used up several of his nine lives. We hope he still has several to go.

1. Write four phrases that describe Buddy.

   _____

   _____

2. How do the people who take care of Buddy feel about him? How can you tell?

   _____

   _____

3. What does it mean when we say that cats have nine lives?

   _____

   _____

Reading Nonfiction

Read the story. Then, answer the questions.

Teeth

Teeth are important for chewing food, so you need to take care of your teeth. When you are a child, you have baby teeth. These fall out and are replaced by adult teeth. You can expect to have a full set of 32 teeth one day. Brush your teeth twice a day, in the morning and at bedtime. Also, floss to remove the bits of food that get stuck between your teeth. That way, you will have a healthy smile!

1. What is the main idea of this story?
   a. You can have a healthy smile.
   b. It is important to take care of your teeth.
   c. Adults have more teeth than children.

2. Why should you take care of your teeth?

   _____

3. What happens to baby teeth?

   _____

4. How many teeth do adults have?

   _____

5. How often should you brush your teeth?
   a. only at lunchtime
   b. once a week
   c. twice a day

Reading Nonfiction

Read the story. Then, answer the questions.

Healthy Heart and Lungs

Your heart and lungs are important parts of your body. The heart moves blood through the body. Without lungs, you could not breathe. You must exercise to keep your heart and lungs healthy. Your heart starts beating faster when you run fast or jump rope. You may breathe harder too. It is good to make your heart and lungs work harder sometimes. This makes them stronger, and you will also feel healthier. Keeping yourself healthy can be a lifelong practice so that you can have a long life.

1. What is the main idea of this story?
   a. Your heart works harder when you run.
   b. Without lungs, you could not breathe.
   c. Exercising keeps your heart and lungs healthy.

2. What does the heart do in the body?

   _____

3. What do lungs help you do?

   _____

4. What happens to your heart when you run fast?
   a. It starts beating faster.
   b. It stops and starts.
   c. It makes you breathe harder.

5. What happens to your lungs when you jump rope?

   _____

6. Why is it good to make your heart work hard sometimes?

   _____

Reading Nonfiction

Read the story. Then, answer the questions.

The Five Senses

Most people have five senses: sight, hearing, smell, taste, and touch. You see with your eyes. You hear with your ears. You smell with your nose. You taste with your tongue, and you touch with your hands. If you have a cold, your sense of smell might not work right. This makes things taste funny too. You want to protect your senses. Keep sharp objects away from your eyes. Turn down the music before it hurts your ears. Never touch a hot stove with your bare hands.

1. What is the main idea of this story?

    _____

2. What are the five senses?

    _____

3. What does your tongue help you do?

    _____

4. What might happen to your senses when you have a cold?

    _____

    _____

5. How can you keep your sense of sight safe?

    _____

6. Why should you not touch a hot stove?

    _____

Reading Nonfiction

Read the story. Then, answer the questions.

Helpful Bugs

Some bugs can destroy crops by eating them. Not all bugs are bad, though. Some bugs even help us. Bees move pollen from one flower to the next. This helps flowers make seeds so that there will be more flowers the next year. Bees also produce honey. Ladybugs are another helpful bug. They eat the bugs that chew on our plants. Finally, spiders may look scary, but they are very helpful bugs. They catch flies, crickets, and moths in their webs. If you find a spider inside the house, ask an adult to help you carefully place it outside. Then, it can do its job.

1. What is the main idea of this story?
   a. Bugs can destroy crops.
   b. Ladybugs are beautiful.
   c. Not all bugs are bad.

2. What do bees produce?
   a. pollen
   b. spiders
   c. honey

3. How do bees help flowers grow?

_____

_____

4. How do ladybugs help us?

_____

5. What do spiders catch in their webs?

_____

Reading Nonfiction

Read the story. Then, answer the questions.

Weather

Weather can be wonderful or very frightening. Rain feels nice on a hot day, but too much rain can cause a flood. People can lose their cars and homes and, sometimes, their lives. A gentle breeze feels good on your skin, but a strong wind can form a tornado, or twister. A tornado can rip the roof off a house. Snow can be fun to play in, but you cannot travel through a snowstorm. If you see a news report that the weather is going to be dangerous, do not be hasty to go outside and watch. It is more fun to watch the weather on TV than to be caught in it!

1. What is the main idea of this story?
   a. You should watch the weather report on the news.
   b. Snow can be fun to play in.
   c. Weather can be wonderful or frightening.

2. What happens when it rains too much?

   _____

3. Why is *twister* a good name for a tornado?

   _____

4. What can a tornado do to a house?

   _____

5. What is hard to do in a snowstorm?

   _____

6. What should you do if the news says the weather is going to be dangerous?

   _____

Name _____

Reading Nonfiction

Read the story. Then, answer the questions.

The Water Cycle

All water on the earth is part of the same cycle. Water starts out in oceans, lakes, and streams. When the sun heats the water, tiny water drops rise into the air. Water in this form is called steam. As the air cools, the water drops form clouds. When the clouds become too heavy with water, they produce rain, sleet, or snow. The rain falls back to the earth. Some of the water goes into the soil, where it helps the plants grow. Some of the water falls into the ocean. Then, the water cycle begins again. The next time you drink a glass of water, think about where it came from!

1. What is the main idea of this story?

   _____

2. Where does the water cycle begin?

   _____

3. What happens when the sun heats the water up?

   _____

4. When do water drops form clouds?

   _____

5. What happens when clouds have too much water?

   _____

6. Where does the rain go after it falls back to the earth?

   _____

Reading Nonfiction

Read the story. Then, answer the questions.

Types of Shelter

    Shelter is a basic human need. People have always built shelter. The type of shelter a group built depended on their needs, the climate, and the materials that were available. Some groups moved around a lot. The people in these groups needed to have homes that they could take with them. Other people who lived in cold places had to build their shelter from ice and snow. All of the groups' shelters served the same purpose of protecting the people who lived in them.

1. What is the main idea of this story?
    a. Shelter is a basic human need that comes in many forms.
    b. Building shelter out of ice is easy.
    c. Different groups had different purposes for shelter.

2. Which two words mean the same thing?
    a. ice and mud
    b. shelter and house
    c. basic and need

3. Why would different groups' shelters look different from each other?

_____

4. Who needed homes they could take with them?

_____

5. What purpose does shelter serve?

_____

Reading Nonfiction

Read the story. Then, answer the questions.

Cities and Towns

Do you know the difference between a city and a town? Usually a city is much larger. In a town, you may have only one school that everyone your age goes to. A city may have many schools for people of the same age. They may have sports teams that play each other for a city title. In a town, you may know most of the other people living there. In a city, you may know only the people on your block or in your building. A city may have more money to provide services, but more people are trying to use those services. There are good and bad things about living in either place.

1. What is the main idea of this story?
   a. Cities are better for young people to live in.
   b. There are good and bad things about life in a town or a city.
   c. People in towns never have any money.

2. How are schools different in cities and towns?

   _____

   _____

3. Who might you know in a town?

   _____

4. Who might you know in a city?

   _____

5. What are some good and bad things about living in a town?

   _____

   _____

Reading Nonfiction

Read the story. Then, answer the questions.

Building a Community

A community is a group of people who care about each other. A community might include your neighbors, school, sports teams, or clubs. People will often offer to help others in their communities. You can be useful to each other. You might decide to walk your neighbor's dog or go to the store for your grandmother. Your uncle might watch your cat while your family goes on vacation. A family down the street might ask you if you want to go to the movies. It is important for people to feel like part of a community. Always be kind and thoughtful to the people in your community, even if you do not know their names.

1. What is the main idea of this story?

_____

2. What people might a community include?

_____

3. How might you help someone in your community?

_____

4. How might someone in your community help you?

_____

5. How should you treat people in your community?

_____

6. Why do people like to feel they are part of a community?

_____

_____

Main Idea

Read the story. Then, answer the questions.

Visiting Grandma and Grandpa

My family likes to visit my grandma and grandpa. They live far away. When we get there, we hug and hug.

My grandpa likes to play with us. He lets us color in his office. He also likes to make bread. We help Grandpa knead the dough.

My grandma keeps lots of cookies and treats in the house. She has lots of books too. Grandma reads to us all day long.

We love to go swimming at Grandma and Grandpa's beach. We bring our rafts and our towels. We can swim all day. Sometimes, we have a picnic. At night, we have a campfire.

Grandma and Grandpa love it when we visit. They are lonely when we are gone. When we drive home, we talk about what we did. I can't wait until we visit again!

1. What is the main idea of the story?

   _____

   _____

2. What do the kids do with their grandma?

   _____

   _____

3. What do the kids do with their grandpa?

   _____

   _____

Main Idea

Read the story. Then, answer the questions.

Staying Cool

Under the hot African sun, two eyes, two ears, and a nose peek out from a cool river. The huge hippopotamus stays in the water all day long. It is too hot out in the sun! The hippo's large body moves easily in the water. The hippo even sleeps in the cool water.

The sun goes down. The hippo comes out of the water to eat. The hippo walks with the other hippos to a nice, grassy spot. They graze for a couple of hours. Then, they go back to the water again.

1. What is the main idea of this passage?

_____

2. On what continent do hippos live?

_____

3. What is the weather like there?

_____

4. How do hippos stay cool?

_____

5. Where do hippos spend most of their time?

_____

6. What do hippos eat?

_____

Main Idea

Read the story. Then, answer the questions.

A Beaver Lodge

A beaver lodge is a home built of sticks in the water. Beaver families are busy all day cutting branches and logs with their front teeth. They carry the branches in their mouths as they swim in the stream. Before they build the lodge, the beavers must find a calm place in a stream or lake. Then, they build a dam with logs and branches. The dam stops the fast water and makes a lake.

The beaver lodge looks like a pile of sticks to us. But under the sticks, the beavers have a cozy home. The beavers get inside the lodge by swimming under the water. Their front door is under the lodge. The lodge is a safe place. Beavers can swim quickly into their home when enemies are near.

1. What is the main idea of this passage?

   _____

2. What do beavers do all day?

   _____

3. Where is the door for the lodge?

   _____

4. What does the dam do?

   _____

5. What is the lodge made of?

   _____

6. How do the beavers carry branches?

   _____

Following Directions

Read the recipe.

Orange Juice Milk Shake

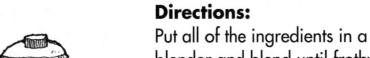

Ingredients:

2 cups (470 ml) orange juice
1 cup (240 ml) milk
4 tablespoons (60 ml) sugar
1 teaspoon (5 ml) vanilla
10 ice cubes

Directions:

Put all of the ingredients in a blender and blend until frothy. Pour into four glasses and serve right away.

Draw the steps for making an orange juice milk shake.

1	2
3	4

Following Directions

Read the recipe.

Worms in Dirt

Ingredients:
2 small boxes of instant chocolate pudding
$3\frac{1}{2}$ cups (830 ml) milk
1 small tub of whipped topping
10 chocolate sandwich cookies
1 bag of gummy worms
8 clear plastic cups

Directions:
In a large bowl, mix pudding and milk until smooth. Stir in the whipped topping. Put the chocolate cookies in a sealed plastic bag. Crush the cookies by rolling them in the bag with a rolling pin.

Put a little pudding in each cup. Put some cookie crumbs on the pudding. Add a little more pudding and sprinkle the rest of the cookie crumbs over the top. Put two gummy worms in each cup.

Draw the steps for making worms in dirt.

1	2	3

4	5	6

Following Directions

Read the story. Then, answer the questions.

Making Bread

The two main ingredients in bread are flour and water. But, there are other important ingredients too. Yeast is very important. Without yeast, a loaf of bread would be flat. A little sugar or honey is needed to feed the yeast so that it will grow and make the bread fluffy. A little salt adds flavor to the bread. Butter or oil makes the bread tender and moist.

After the ingredients are mixed together, the bread dough is kneaded. To knead, you punch, push, fold, and pinch the dough. Kneading may take 15 minutes. The bread must rest in a warm place for an hour or two so that it can rise. Then, you can shape the bread into loaves. Before it bakes, the bread rises again until it is twice as big as when you started.

When bread is baking, the house smells wonderful. It is hard to wait until it is done!

1. What does yeast do to bread?

_____

2. What does salt add to bread?

_____

3. How do you knead the dough?

_____

4. What are the ingredients in bread?

_____

Vocabulary

Read the story. Then, answer the questions.

Wash Your Hands

You have most likely heard your family and teachers tell you to wash your hands. Be sure to use warm water and soap. Rub your hands together for as long as it takes to sing the ABCs. Then, sing the song again while you rinse them. Soap can help kill the germs, or tiny bugs, that make you sick. If you do not wash your hands, you can pass along an illness to a friend. You could also spread the germs to your eyes or mouth if you touch them before washing your hands. Remember to wash your hands!

1. What is the main idea of this story?
   a. Bugs can make you sick.
   b. Rub your hands together.
   c. You should wash your hands with warm water and soap.

2. How long should you rub your hands together?

   _____

3. What does soap do?

   _____

4. What does the word *germs* mean?
   a. kinds of soap
   b. tiny bugs that can make you sick
   c. ways to wash your hands

5. What could happen if you don't wash your hands?

   _____

Vocabulary

Read the story. Then, answer the questions.

The Beach

Have you ever been to the beach? It is fun to play in the sand and then wash off in the water. Tiny fish might tickle your feet when you walk into the ocean. Birds called pelicans fly in circles above the water. When they see a fish move, they dive to catch it. Crabs hurry along the shoreline. You may find seashells in the sand. If you go to a harbor, you will see ships as well as seagulls. The gulls like to eat food that people have thrown away. They are nature's garbage collectors!

1. What is the main idea of this story?
   a. There is a lot to see at the beach.
   b. Crabs hurry along the shoreline.
   c. Seagulls like to eat trash.

2. What can you do at the beach?

   _____

   _____

3. Why do pelicans fly in circles?

   _____

   _____

4. What other animals besides pelicans might you find at the beach?

   _____

5. What does the word *harbor* mean?
   a. nature's garbage collectors
   b. a type of seagull
   c. a place where ships unload their goods

Vocabulary

Read the story. Then, answer the questions.

The Right to Vote

Have you ever voted for class president? Maybe your class has cast votes for the best movie star or type of ice cream. Voting for members of the government is very important. In the United States and Canada, you have to be 18 to vote in one of these elections. Not everyone has been able to vote in the past. In the United States, women were not allowed to vote until 1920. A special law was passed in 1965 to make sure that all adult citizens get to vote. When you vote, you have a say in who serves in the government and what kinds of laws they pass. Some people say that voting is the most important thing that people can do.

1. What is the main idea of this story?
   a. Chocolate ice cream is the best.
   b. Not everyone can vote in the United States.
   c. Voting is an important thing for people to be able to do.

2. Who can vote in the United States and Canada?

   _____

3. What happens in an election?

   a. People cast votes.
   b. People have to be 18.
   c. People pass laws.

4. When were US women first allowed to vote?

   _____

5. What happened in the United States after a special law was passed in 1965?

   _____

6. Why is voting important?

   _____

Text Features

> **Charts** and **tables** are helpful in organizing information. To read a chart, match the given information from the top and side to find new information in the boxes.
>
> Example: *Who will use the science center on Friday?*
>
> Look at the chart below. Find the science center along the side and follow the row to Friday. You will find Kendra's name in the box.

Centers	Monday	Tuesday	Wednesday	Thursday	Friday
Reading	Sandie	Elena	Sam	Kendra	Evan
Listening	Elena	Sam	Kendra	Evan	Sandie
Math	Sam	Kendra	Evan	Sandie	Elena
Art	Kendra	Evan	Sandie	Elena	Sam
Science	Evan	Sandie	Elena	Sam	Kendra

Use the information from the chart to find the answers.

1. Who will use the art center on Thursday? _____

2. What center will Sam use on Monday? _____

3. On what day will Evan use the science center? _____

4. What center will Sandie use on Friday? _____

5. Who will use the reading center on Wednesday? _____

6. On what day will Elena use the math center? _____

Text Features

Read the table of contents. Then, answer the questions.

All about Bears

1. What chapter tells about how bears act in the zoo?

   _____

2. What chapter might tell you how big a baby bear is?

   _____

3. On what page does the chapter on grizzly bears start?

   _____

4. What chapter will tell you how big brown bears are?

   _____

5. Could you read about bear food on page 38?

   _____

6. On what page does the chapter about bears and people begin?

   _____

7. Will this book tell you about a teddy bear that lost a button? Why or why not?

   _____

Text Features

> Most chapter books and longer informational books have a **table of contents** page after the title page. This helps you find parts of the book more quickly.

Your teacher has asked you to write a report about animals. In the report, you must answer all of the questions listed below. It would take you a very long time to read the entire book, so you decide to use the table of contents to help you. Write the chapter and page number where you would begin looking to answer each question.

Table of Contents

Animals Around the World

	Chapter to look in	Page to begin looking
1. How long do lions live?		
2. How fast do sailfish swim?		
3. What do snakes eat?		
4. How long does it take for robin eggs to hatch?		
5. Do spiders bite?		
6. Where do poison dart frogs live?		
7. What do beavers eat?		
8. How long do turtles live?		

Author's Purpose

Read the story. Then, answer the questions.

Moving

   I packed my toys. I put my clothes in a box. My books are coming too. I said good-bye to my room. I said good-bye to my swing set. I said good-bye to my friends. I do not want to go.

   My new house is big. I have my own room. I hope my mom remembered my bike. There are kids next door. I wonder if they know how to play hide-and-seek. I am glad to be here.

Draw a picture of the child at the old house and at the new house. Show what the child does at each house.

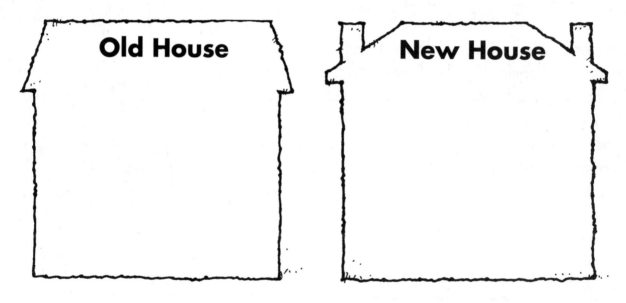

Old House   **New House**

1. Why did the author write this story?_____

_____

2. What do you think is bad about moving? _____

3. What do you think is good about moving? _____

Author's Purpose

Read the story. Then, circle the correct answer to each question.

Charades

Have you ever played charades? Charades is a fun game to play with a large group of friends. All you need to play is a pencil and paper.

Split the group into two teams. Each team writes down book, movie, and song titles on little pieces of paper. The pieces of paper are then put into two bowls. One person takes a piece of paper from the other team's bowl. That person must act out the title. Her team has to guess what the title is.

First, the player shows the team whether it is a movie, song, or book. The player cannot talk or make sounds. Only hand and body motions are allowed. The player shows how many words are in the title. Then, the team watches the player act out the words. They guess and shout out their answers.

Everyone gets a turn. Both teams play. The winner is the team that guesses the most titles.

1. What is the reason this article was written?
    to make you laugh   to teach you   to get you to buy something

2. What do you need to play charades?
    a game board   money   paper and a pencil

3. How many people can play the game?
    two   three   a crowd

4. What do players write on their papers?
    their names   funny stories   titles

5. What can't you use when you play charades?
    your pencil   your voice   your hands

Author's Purpose

Read the story. Then, answer the questions.

Bridges

There are different kinds of bridges. Arch bridges are long. Beam bridges are short. Beam bridges may help people drive over rivers or other roads. Arch bridges are very strong. They may help people drive over small lakes or mountain valleys. Other bridges hang from strong wires. They are called suspension bridges and can be even longer than arch bridges.

1. Which bridge is strong?

_____

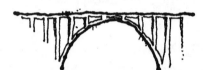

2. Where do beam bridges go?

_____

3. Where do arch bridges go?

_____

4. What are bridges for?

_____

_____

5. What kinds of bridges have you seen?

_____

6. What is the author's purpose for writing this passage?

_____

Reading Graphs

Water or Juice?

The students in Mr. Burr's second-grade class made a graph. Each student put a block on the graph. Look at the finished graph and answer the questions.

Would you rather drink water or juice?

Water ▪▪▪▪▪▪

Juice ▪▪▪▪▪▪▪▪▪▪▪▪▪▪▪▪▪

1. How many students chose juice? _____

2. How many students chose water? _____

3. How many more students chose juice than water? _____

4. How many students total are in the class? _____

5. Does the graph tell what kind of juice the students like? _____

Reading Graphs

Favorite Frozen Treats

Marjorie asked the kids in her class to name their favorite frozen treats. Then, she made a graph to show the results.

FAVORITE FROZEN TREATS

Number of Kids

10
9
8
7
6
5
4
3
2
1
0

fudge bars   frozen juice bars   ice-cream cones   red, white, and blue bars

Kinds of Treats

Read the graph. Then, answer the questions.

1. How many kids like ice-cream cones best? _____

2. How many kids like fudge bars best? _____

3. How many more kids like frozen juice bars than red, white, and blue bars? _____

4. Does the graph tell you how many kids Marjorie asked? _____

   If yes, how many? _____

Reading Graphs

Read the graph. Then, answer the questions.

How Much Pizza?

1. How many pieces of pizza are there?

   _____

2. Which two people can eat half a pizza together?

   _____

   _____

3. Who eats more pizza, Peter or Julia?

   _____

4. Does the graph tell you what is on the pizza?

   _____

   If yes, what?

   _____

5. Does the graph tell you who eats the most pizza?

   _____

   If yes, who?

   _____

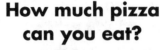

How much pizza can you eat?

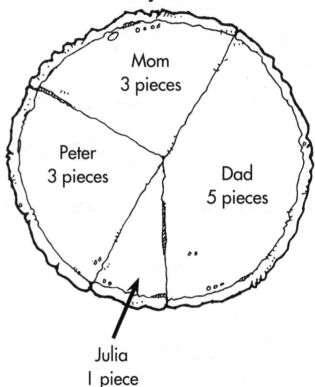

Mom
3 pieces

Peter
3 pieces

Dad
5 pieces

Julia
1 piece

Compare and Contrast

Read the story. Then, answer the questions.

Sisters

My big sister loves to talk. She talks about what she sees and does. She reads books when she is not talking. She talks about what she reads. She reads about people, animals, and places. I like to listen to her. I am quiet. I like to close my eyes and see pictures in my head. I can see the things my sister talks about. I like to draw pictures, too. My sister likes to look at my pictures. She thinks I am smart. I think she is smart.

1. Which sister is more like you? _____

2. What do you like to do best? _____

Use the details from the story to fill in the Venn diagram.

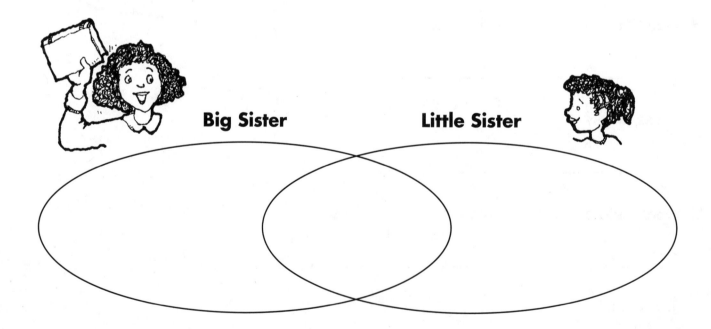

Big Sister   **Little Sister**

Compare and Contrast

Read the recipes.

Play Dough

Play Dough #1

Ingredients:
1 cup (240 ml) flour
$\frac{1}{2}$ cup (120 ml) salt
1 cup (240 ml) water
2 tablespoons (30 ml) cooking oil
2 teaspoons (10 ml) cream of tartar
  food coloring

Directions:
Mix the ingredients in a large pot. Cook and stir until a ball forms. Let it cool. Mix the dough with your hands.

Play Dough #2

Ingredients:
$1\frac{3}{4}$ cups (410 ml) water
$2\frac{1}{2}$ cups (590 ml) flour
$\frac{1}{2}$ cup (120 ml) salt
2 tablespoons (30 ml) cooking oil
2 tablespoons (30 ml) alum
  food coloring

Directions:
Boil the water. Mix with the other ingredients in a bowl. Stir until a ball forms. Let it cool. Mix the dough with your hands.

Circle the best answers. Write the other answers on the lines.

1. Which recipe do you think makes more play dough?   #1   #2

   Why? _____

2. Which play dough needs to be cooked?   #1   #2

3. Which ingredient in the second recipe is not in the first recipe?

   alum   oil   flour

4. Which ingredients are in both recipes?

   alum   oil   flour   salt

   cream of tartar   water   food coloring

5. Why don't the recipes tell what color food coloring to use?

   _____

Compare and Contrast

Read the story. Then, fill in the Venn diagram.

Alligators and Crocodiles

Is that a log in the water? It doesn't seem to be moving. But, aren't those eyes? Watch out! It's an alligator! Or, is it a crocodile? Many people confuse alligators and crocodiles. They look and act very much the same.

Alligators and crocodiles live in the water. They eat fish, turtles, birds, and other animals. Crocodiles have pointed snouts. Alligators have wide, rounded snouts. The upper jaw of the alligator is wider than its lower jaw. When an alligator's mouth is closed, you cannot see many of its teeth. The upper and lower jaws of the crocodile are about the same size. You can see many of its teeth when its mouth is closed. The fourth tooth on the bottom jaw sticks up over the upper lip.

Crocodiles and alligators are cold-blooded. This means that both animals stay cool in the water and warm up in the sun. Alligators prefer to be in freshwater. Crocodiles are often found in salt water. You may think alligators and crocodiles are slow because they lie so still in the water. But, they can move fast on land with their short legs. Both animals are very fierce. Stay away! They may be quietly watching for YOU!

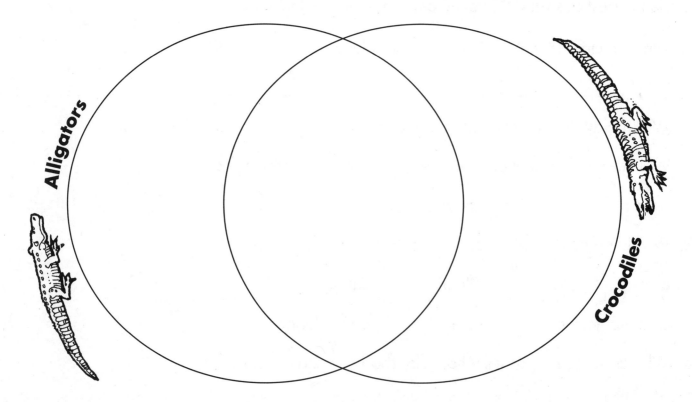

Long and Short Vowels

When two vowels are together, the first one usually makes its long sound, and the second one is usually silent.

Look at these double vowel words:

road faint
rōd fānt

Watch for the vowel *i* to be followed by the silent *gh*:

night
nīt

Circle the word that names each picture.

1. hear / hay	2. paint / pant	3. weed / wed
4. bet / beet	5. light / lit	6. fit / fight
7. paid / pad	8. rough / right	9. cot / coat
10. coast / cost	11. beads / beds	12. met / meat
13. goat / got	14. red / read	15. tray / train

Long and Short Vowels

Look at the words in the list below. Sort the words into two groups, one with long vowel sounds and one with short vowel sounds.

gate	goat	wheat	pack
frog	sock	rug	time
egg	own	gum	man
cue	rate	nest	fine

Long Vowel Sounds   **Short Vowel Sounds**

_____   _____

_____   _____

_____   _____

_____   _____

_____   _____

_____   _____

_____   _____

_____   _____

Long and Short Vowels

Look at the words in the list below. Sort the words into two groups, one with long vowel sounds and one with short vowel sounds.

mice	phone	top	blue
ear	mat	face	most
nose	light	fog	nap
pen	long	track	feet
duck	red	sit	cup
fuss	tube	paste	mine

Long Vowel Sounds   **Short Vowel Sounds**

_____   _____

_____   _____

_____   _____

_____   _____

_____   _____

_____   _____

_____   _____

_____   _____

_____   _____

_____   _____

R-Controlled Vowels

When a vowel is followed by the letter *r*, it makes a new sound. Say these words to hear the *r*-controlled vowel sounds:

  car   bird   fern   church   corn

Circle the word that names each picture.

1. park pork	2. bride bird	3. born barn	4. dirt dart
5. farm firm	6. porch perch	7. starve serve	8. cord card
9. warm worm	10. stark stork	11. fern firm	12. third tired **3rd**
13. girl grill	14. short shirt	15. three thirty **30**	16. burn born
17. press purse	18. turn torn	19. fur for	20. heart hurt

Name _____

R-Controlled Vowels

Look at the words in the list below. Sort the words with *ur* or *ar* into the first two groups. Look at the letters of the remaining words and label a third group. Write the words that belong in each group.

burr	artist	feather	return
power	part	shark	dancer
hunger	card	center	furry
turn	purpose	yard	farm
super	surprise	suffer	yarn
start	century	writer	slurp

ur Sound   **ar Sound**   _____

_____   _____   _____

_____   _____   _____

_____   _____   _____

_____   _____   _____

_____   _____   _____

_____   _____   _____

_____   _____   _____

2.RF.3b

R-Controlled Vowels

Look at the words in the list below. Write the words with *or* in the first group. Look at the letters of the remaining words and label the second and third groups. Write the words that belong in each group.

darkness	storm	during	form
fork	burn	department	born
cartoon	purple	party	nurse
stork	turn	torn	sharp
curl	star	hurry	park
market	worn	doctor	fur

or Sound _____ _____

_____   _____   _____

_____   _____   _____

_____   _____   _____

_____   _____   _____

_____   _____   _____

_____   _____   _____

_____   _____   _____

Reading Poetry

Practice reading the poem aloud with fluency and expression. Then, answer the questions.

Chook, Chook

Chook, chook, chook, chook, chook.
Good morning, Mrs. Hen.
How many chickens have you got?
Madam, I've got ten.
Four of them are yellow,
And four of them are brown,
And two of them are speckled red,
The nicest in the town.
by Anonymous

1. In this poem, Mrs. Hen proudly tells about her chicks. Draw the chicks in the picture above just as she describes them.

2. Fill in the graph to show how many chicks she has of each color.

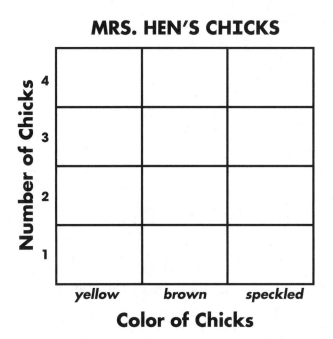

MRS. HEN'S CHICKS

Number of Chicks

4

3

2

1

yellow   brown   speckled

Color of Chicks

Reading Poetry

Practice reading the poem aloud with fluency and expression. Have a friend time you for one minute. Record the number of words you read correctly in one minute.

What Animal Is It?

Whisky, frisky,
Hippity hop,
Up he goes,
To the treetop!
Whirly, twirly,
Round and round,
Down he scampers,
To the ground.
Furly, curly,
What a tail!
Tall as a feather,
Broad as a sail.
Where's his supper?
In the shell,
Snappity, crackity,
Out it fell!
by Anonymous

_____ words per minute

Reading Poetry

Practice reading the poem aloud with fluency and expression. Have a friend time you for one minute. Record the number of words you read correctly in one minute.

Wheels

Bikes have two wheels,
Tricycles three.
Scooters have two wheels.
Watch me! Whee!

I like to roller-skate.
It's a piece of cake.
I can do tricks.
Let's hit the bricks.

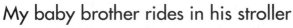

My baby brother rides in his stroller
While I'm on my bike.
We roll down the sidewalk in the sun.
My brother laughs at me riding.
He thinks it's fun
To see his sister smiling
And hear my bell tinkling
And feel my streamers flapping in his face.

_____ words per minute

Reading Fluently

Practice reading the passage aloud with fluency and expression. Have a friend time you for one minute. Record the number of words you read correctly in one minute.

Stolen Bike

Adam ran into the house. "Mom, my bike is gone!"

Mom said calmly, "Let's go look for it together."

"Mom, I know I left it right here in the garage last night," said Adam.

Mom and Adam looked in all the places the bike could be. Then, Mom called the police.

A few minutes later, a black and white car drove up. The police officer asked Adam questions about his bike. Adam answered the questions.

The officer said, "You should keep the garage door closed." He told Adam he would call them if he found the bike. The police car drove away.

Mom said, "Let's go shopping at garage sales. Maybe we can find a used bike for you."

_____ words per minute

Reading Fluently

Practice reading the passage aloud with fluency and expression. Have a friend time you for one minute. Record the number of words you read correctly in one minute.

Playing Outside

Annie and Charlie played outside. The morning sun felt warm on Annie's head. She could smell the flowers that grew next to the house. She picked some ripe strawberries and shared two with Charlie. Annie laughed when Charlie smeared the berries on his cheek and chin.

Charlie played in the sandbox. He pushed the truck in the sand and made a noise with his lips. Later, he pointed at the swing. Annie picked Charlie up and set him in the red swing. She put on his seat belt and gave him a gentle push. Charlie laughed. Annie sat on the swing next to him and counted the 10 red flowers by the house. "When I grow up, I want to take care of plants," said Annie.

"More!" said Charlie. Annie got up and pushed the swing.

"It's almost time for lunch," said Annie. "Mom is making us a picnic. Are you hungry?"

"More!" said Charlie.

_____ words per minute

Reading Fluently

Practice reading the passage aloud with fluency and expression. Have a friend time you for one minute. Record the number of words you read correctly in one minute.

Missing Pen Mystery

Mrs. Flores asked her students if they had seen her favorite blue pen with stars on it. Joseph looked at Kyle and whispered, "It sounds like a mystery."

At recess break, Joseph talked to Mrs. Flores. "May we look at the crime scene?" There was a brown spot on the clean desk.

Kyle asked Mrs. Flores if she had eaten any chocolate that day.

"No," sighed Mrs. Flores, "but I wish I had some now."

Joseph looked in the trash can. The boys looked at all of the students' faces as they walked in the door.

After school, the boys went to see Mr. Burk. Mr. Burk loved chocolate. Kyle and Joseph saw Mr. Burk in the hallway. He had a blue pen in his pocket.

"Is that your pen, Mr. Burk?" asked Joseph.

"Well, no," he said as he patted his pocket. "I borrowed it from someone."

"Did you find it on Mrs. Flores's desk?" asked Kyle.

"Yes, I did. I guess I better give it back to her."

"Case closed," said the boys.

_____ words per minute

Reading Fluently

Read the passage aloud. Have a friend time you for one minute. Record the number of words you read correctly in one minute. Practice reading with expression.

Worm Bins

Did you know that worms can eat your garbage? Worms are busy eaters. They eat leftover food, grass, and leaves. Their bodies turn the food into rich soil. You can use that soil to make your garden grow better.

Some people keep worms in a large box. The box is called a worm bin. The worm bin is full of newspaper bits, grass, and leaves. People put their apple peelings, eggshells, and vegetable ends in the worm bin. The worms will eat happily and make soil.

It is not a good idea to put meat in the worm bin. Worms will not eat meat very quickly, and the meat will start to smell bad. Worms cannot eat plastic, foil, or wood. They just eat the food that you usually throw away.

There are two great things about starting a worm bin. You will have less garbage to throw away, and you will have great soil for your garden.

_____ words per minute

Reading Fluently

Read the passage aloud. Have a friend time you for one minute. Record the number of words you read correctly in one minute. Don't forget to read with expression!

Snowboarding

What sport can make you feel like you are flying? Try snowboarding. It's a little like surfing. It's a little like skateboarding. It's a little like skiing too. To snowboard, you stand on one board and glide down a snowy hill very quickly. A snowboard is shaped kind of like a skateboard, but it is longer and wider. It does not have wheels. It is made of fiberglass, wood, and metal. Snowboards come in many shapes, sizes, and colors. A beginner usually uses a short, wide board.

Snowboarders wear special boots that snap onto the snowboard. Most people ride with their left feet in front. Their toes point in a little. You can turn the board by leaning on your toes or heels. Turning on a snowboard is called edging.

Like any new sport, snowboarding takes lots of practice. Many ski resorts allow people to snowboard on their slopes. But before they do, snowboarders must learn safety tips and rules.

Expert snowboarders can do special tricks. These people are very skilled. They are not beginners. They can ride backwards. They can spin or do a wheelie, an ollie, or a grab. There are many tricks, but some experts just want to go fast down a mountain.

_____ words per minute

Reading Fluently

Read the passage aloud. Have a friend time you for one minute. Record the number of words you read correctly in one minute. Don't forget to read with expression!

Birthday Fun

Marissa's eighth birthday party was a hit! Her friends said it was the best party ever. Marissa's birthday was in March. It was cold outside. But inside, Marissa's basement was hot. It was a beach party!

Everybody brought a bathing suit and beach towel. The children laid their towels on the floor and put on suntan lotion. At first, they had fun building a sand castle. They used cardboard boxes and sandpaper.

Later, everyone changed into regular clothes and played some games. The first game was pin the leg on the octopus. Each person wore a blindfold and tried to pin a leg onto a picture of an octopus. Ambi pinned the leg closest to the octopus. She won the game.

The next game was a crab race. The children raced in pairs. They had to crawl backwards on their hands and feet. Max was the fastest of all of the kids.

After the games, each guest decorated a pair of sunglasses. They used shells, glitter, feathers, and markers. Everyone looked pretty cool.

At snack time, the kids had hot dogs, blue gelatin dessert with gummy sharks, and lemonade. The cake looked like a beach. It was decorated with a sun, water, and sand. There was shell candy on the sand and a gummy shark in the water.

When it was time to go, everyone got a beach pail full of candy and toys. Too bad they had to put on their warm coats and boots to go back outside!

_____ words per minute

Reading Fluently

Read the passage aloud. Have a friend time you for one minute. Record the number of words you read correctly in one minute. Don't forget to read with expression!

Jennifer's Family

Jennifer Hall was adopted by her mom and dad. Jennifer was just a baby when she was adopted. She is eight years old now. She had parents who gave birth to her. Her birth parents loved her, but they had problems. They could not take care of her.

Mr. and Mrs. Hall wanted a family. They wanted to adopt a baby. They went to a social worker who helped them find Jennifer. When she was very little, Jennifer came to live with her mom and dad. Jennifer loved her new family right away. They loved her too.

Jennifer's mom and dad went to a courtroom and said that they wanted to become her parents. They promised to love her and take care of her. The judge signed some papers. Jennifer had a new family. They will be a family forever.

_____ words per minute

Reading Fluently

Read the passage aloud. Have a friend time you for one minute. Record the number of words you read correctly in one minute. Don't forget to read with expression!

Lost at Sea

The *Titanic* was a huge ship. It was the biggest ship in the world. The *Titanic* was built to sail across the ocean. The boat had dining rooms, a pool, nine decks, and a gym. The ship was like a moving city.

Many people bought tickets for the *Titanic's* first trip. Everyone was excited. The ship sailed for three days. Then, it hit an iceberg. The ice punched holes in the side of the ship. Water began to fill the hull.

Slowly, the ship sank. There were not enough lifeboats for everyone. Many people got into lifeboats. Other people died in the water. The giant ship broke in half and sank to the bottom of the ocean.

Seventy years later, scientists found the *Titanic*. The ship was rusted and broken. The scientists took many pictures. They did not take anything away from the ship. The scientists put a plaque on the ship. The plaque is in memory of the people who died.

_____ words per minute

Reading Fluently

Read the passage aloud. Have a friend time you for one minute. Record the number of words you read correctly in one minute. Don't forget to read with expression!

Return Top

You know what a top is, right? A top is a toy that spins on the floor. Do you know what a "return top" is? You probably do. It's a yo-yo.

To play with a yo-yo, you should first make sure that the string is the right length. When the yo-yo is unwound and near the floor, your hand should be about 3 inches (7 cm) above your waist. If the string is too long, cut it.

Tie a slipknot at the end of the string. A slipknot is a loop that will fit any size finger. Slip the loop around your middle finger at the first joint. Wind the string and hold the yo-yo in your hand. Then, open your hand and toss the yo-yo with a jerk. The yo-yo will unwind and then wind back up. It returns to your hand.

Now, it is time to learn a trick. The basic trick is "the sleeper." Throw the yo-yo a little softer, and it will unwind and stay spinning near the floor. Give it a little jerk. It will come back to you. Try to let it sleep for a count of five. Keep practicing. You have to move your wrist just right.

Yo-yo experts can do many tricks. "Walk the dog" and "around the world" are very popular tricks. The biggest yo-yo ever spun was dropped from a crane. Maybe you can invent a new trick!

_____ words per minute

Plural Nouns

A **noun** can be singular (one person, place, or thing) or **plural** (more than one).

Circle the correct noun in each sentence.

1. The three (school, schools) are on the same street.

2. Two (cat, cats) climbed up the tree.

3. The (crab, crabs) has sharp claws.

4. Many (bush, bushes) have berries on them.

5. There are two (Julio, Julios) in my class.

6. That (boy, boys) waved at you.

7. One (doctor, doctors) left for the day.

8. A (tree, trees) can have many leaves on it.

Plural Nouns

Use the plural forms of the nouns to fill in the sentences.

   Example: penny   cup

   *There are six **pennies** in the two **cups**.*

1. mouse   room

   There are two _____ in the three _____.

2. child   bench

   There are four _____ on the two _____.

3. blueberry   dish

   There are five _____ in the two _____.

4. nut   box

   There are six _____ in the four _____.

Plural Nouns

A noun can be singular or plural. Some nouns become plural by making changes in the middles or at the ends.

Draw lines to match the singular and plural nouns.

goose	children
mouse	people
tooth	feet
child	leaves
foot	women
person	mice
man	geese
woman	halves
leaf	men
half	teeth

Circle the plural nouns in each sentence.

1. We cut the candy bars into halves.

2. Men, women, and children are all people.

3. A goose has two feet. Four geese have eight feet.

4. Mice have sharp teeth.

5. Many leaves are on that tree.

Sentences

> A **sentence** is a group of words that tells a complete thought. A sentence always starts with an uppercase letter.

Rewrite the sentences. Start each sentence with an uppercase letter. Circle the uppercase letter at the beginning of each sentence.

1. i like studying grammar.

   _____

2. mary will underline nouns with yellow.

   _____

3. sandy and Kit underline verbs with blue.

   _____

4. janice circled the first noun in the sentence.

   _____

   _____

Sentences

A **sentence** is a group of words that tells a complete thought. A sentence always starts with an uppercase letter.

Circle the first letter of each sentence. Write an uppercase letter above each lowercase letter that needs to be changed.

1. in the afternoon, we learn about science.

2. i get to school at 8:45 am.

3. i sit down at my desk.

4. olivia helps with the calendar.

5. my pencil breaks during math.

6. ms. Acker reads a great book.

7. the class eats lunch.

8. we clean out our messy desks.

9. ryan picks me up after school.

10. ms. Acker will teach us about volcanoes tomorrow.

Sentences

> A **sentence** is a group of words that tells a complete thought. A sentence always starts with an uppercase letter and ends with a punctuation mark.

Add words to make each group of words a complete sentence. Start each sentence with an uppercase letter and end each sentence with the correct punctuation mark.

1. runs to

_____

2. will Dean

_____

3. get a

_____

4. the brown cow

_____

5. begins at noon

_____

Underline the nouns in each of the sentences.

Proper Nouns

Days, months, and holidays are **proper nouns**. A proper noun always starts with an uppercase letter.

Look at the words. Cross out the first letter of each proper noun and write an uppercase letter above it.

1. st. patrick's day	monday	thanksgiving
2. friday	sunday	july
3. new year's day	august	hearts
4. hanukkah	turkey	january
5. saturday	february	christmas
6. october	calendar	november
7. tuesday	leprechaun	december
8. wednesday	valentine's day	thursday

Proper Nouns

Days and months are **proper nouns**. Some of these nouns can be abbreviated, or shortened. The complete words and their abbreviations always start with uppercase letters.

Draw lines to match the nouns that name days and months to their abbreviations. (Some months do not have abbreviations.)

Tuesday	Thurs.	January	Sept.
Friday	Sat.	February	Apr.
Sunday	Tues.	March	Oct.
Thursday	Fri.	April	Dec.
Wednesday	Sun.	August	Jan.
Monday	Wed.	September	Aug.
Saturday	Mon.	October	Mar.
		November	Feb.
		December	Nov.

Beginning with *Sunday*, write the days of the week in order. Start each word with an uppercase letter.

1. _____

2. _____

3. _____

4. _____

5. _____

6. _____

7. _____

Proper Nouns

Proper nouns name specific people, places, and things. A proper noun always starts with an uppercase letter. When proper nouns name a city and state, a comma goes between them.

Example: *Orlando, Florida*

Write the names and addresses correctly. Capitalize the proper nouns. Put a comma between each city name and state name.

1. mr. cody stoneson
   461 oak avenue
   littletown ohio 12345

   _____

   _____

   _____

2. dr. coral sargasso
   876 waterway boulevard
   kelp maine 13579

   _____

   _____

   _____

Draw an X next to each proper noun that names a person.

Contractions

A **contraction** is two words that are put together to make one word. Some of the letters drop out of the second word when the words are joined. An apostrophe takes the place of the dropped letters.

Example: *did + not = didn't*

Draw lines to match the word pairs with their contractions.

are not	couldn't
were not	isn't
could not	aren't
did not	haven't
do not	wasn't
have not	don't
is not	didn't
was not	weren't

Write a contraction on the line to finish each sentence.

1. We _____ going to the circus tonight.
   are not

2. Gerard _____ play basketball today.
   did not

3. It _____ raining outside now.
   is not

4. You _____ need a jacket.
   do not

Contractions

A **contraction** is two words that are put together to make one word. Some of the letters drop out of the second word when the words are joined. An apostrophe takes the place of the dropped letters.

Draw lines to match the word pairs with their contractions.

he is	she's
I would	he'd
she is	they've
you have	I'm
we are	let's
he would	I've
they have	he's
they are	you're
I am	what's
what is	you've
you are	I'd
I have	they're
let us	we're

Contractions

A **contraction** is two words that are put together to make one word. Some of the letters drop out of the second word when the words are joined. Sometimes the words' letters change to make the contraction. An apostrophe takes the place of the dropped letters.

Write a contraction on the line to finish each sentence.

1. Jill _____ climb that enormous tree.
   will not

2. The sign says _____ need a green ticket to get in.
   you will

3. I think _____ eating a hot dinner soon.
   we are

4. _____ the recipe for bread dough?
   What is

5. That _____ the fourth bell.
   was not

6. _____ ridden the yellow bus to school.
   She had

7. _____ feeding the two hamsters this week?
   Who is

On another sheet of paper, write a story about climbing a tree. Use contractions in your story.

Compound Words

> Sometimes two words can be put together to make a new word with its own meaning. This new word is called a **compound word**.
>
> Example: *farm + house = farmhouse*

Write each word pair as a compound word.

1. sun + light = _____

2. birth + day = _____

3. every + one = _____

4. rain + bow = _____

5. water + melon = _____

6. bare + foot = _____

7. home + work = _____

8. mid + night = _____

9. rail + road = _____

Compound Words

Sometimes two words can be put together to make a new word with its own meaning. This new word is called a **compound word**.

Write each word pair as a compound word.

1. after + noon = _____

2. back + yard = _____

3. class + mate = _____

4. break + fast = _____

5. flash + light = _____

6. oat + meal = _____

7. pop + corn = _____

Use a compound word from above to finish each sentence.

8. Nate saw fireflies in his _____.

9. Ricky will need a _____ when he camps outside.

10. Claire likes to eat _____ at the movies with her grandmother.

Underline the other compound words in the sentences.

Compound Words

Sometimes two words can be put together to make a new word with its own meaning. This new word is called a **compound word**.

Write a compound word on the line to finish each sentence.

1. Amy plays _____ at the park.

2. We found a _____ on the beach.

3. We saw a beautiful _____ after the storm.

4. Will you come to my _____ party on Sunday?

5. Taylor likes to eat _____ at the movies.

6. We camped out in my _____ last night.

7. Does your teacher give you _____ every night?

8. The train travels on a _____ track.

9. You should eat a good _____ every morning.

10. _____ had a great time at the pool.

On another sheet of paper, write a story about going to the beach. Include as many compound words as you can.

Using a Dictionary

> A dictionary is a book full of words and their meanings. To make it easier to find a particular word, the entire dictionary is written in alphabetical order.

The words below belong in a dictionary. Write each group in alphabetical order.

might	evening	boil
carp	magnet	icicle

1. _____   4. _____

2. _____   5. _____

3. _____   6. _____

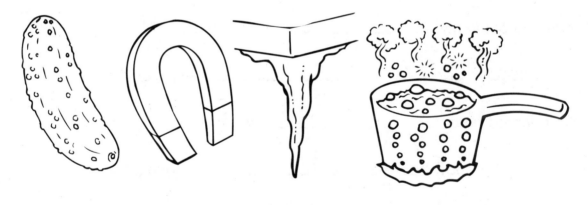

height	pickle	diet
drain	frisky	practice

1. _____   4. _____

2. _____   5. _____

3. _____   6. _____

Using a Dictionary

Use this part of a dictionary to answer the questions.

> **mend** — to heal
> **pastime** — a hobby
> **stalk** — a large stem
>
> **tragic** — sad
> **wrench** — a tool used to tighten a bolt

1. Where would you find a stalk growing?

   a. at the mall   b. in a bathroom   c. on TV   d. in a cornfield

2. How do you spell the word that means sad?

   a. gratic   b. tragic   c. cragit   d. tagric

3. Who would use a wrench?

   a. a nurse   b. a cook   c. a repair person   d. a baseball player

Use the words to answer the questions.

> stork   petunia   hammer   bushel   candle

4. If these words were found in a dictionary, which would be first?

   a. stork   b. candle   c. bushel   d. hammer

5. Which word would be last?

   a. stork   b. candle   c. bushel   d. hammer

Using a Dictionary

A **dictionary** is a book full of words and their meanings. The word you look up is called the **entry word** and its meaning is called a **definition**.

Use the definitions to label each picture with its matching entry word.

angle — shape formed by two lines meeting at a common point
parallel — two lines that never cross
perpendicular — two lines that cross at right angles to make a "+"
point — a dot
ray — a point with a line that goes only one way
segment — two points with a line between them

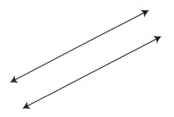

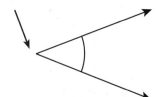

1. _____

2. _____

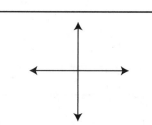

3. _____

4. _____

5. _____

6. _____

Synonyms

Read the story below. Decide which word in the box has almost the same meaning as each underlined word in the story. Write your answers on the lines.

contests	burning	go	enjoy
unhappy	playground	chilly	

Summer

I $\underset{1}{\underline{like}}$ summer. My friends and I play $\underset{2}{\underline{games}}$ at the $\underset{3}{\underline{park}}$. The sun is $\underset{4}{\underline{hot}}$, but the pool is $\underset{5}{\underline{cool}}$. We are $\underset{6}{\underline{sad}}$ when it is time to $\underset{7}{\underline{leave}}$.

1. _____   5. _____

2. _____   6. _____

3. _____   7. _____

4. _____

Draw a picture to go with the story.

Name _____

Synonyms

Read the story below. Decide which word in the box has almost the same meaning as each underlined word or phrase in the story. Write your answers on the lines.

```
   takes        each       bright      pals
 neighbor       good       stormy     travel
```

Going to School

My <u>friends</u>¹ and I <u>go</u>² to school in different ways. Trey's mother <u>drives</u>³ him in her black truck. Jan rides the bus with a <u>girl next door</u>⁴. Tara and Miguel walk to school if the weather is <u>nice</u>⁵. I ride my bicycle <u>every</u>⁶ day whether it is <u>rainy</u>⁷ or <u>sunny</u>⁸!

1. _____   5. _____

2. _____   6. _____

3. _____   7. _____

4. _____   8. _____

Draw a picture to go with the story.

Synonyms

Read the story below. Decide which word in the box has almost the same meaning as each underlined word or phrase in the story. Write your answers on the lines.

pick	large	spotless	box	hop
small	vacation	crying	just	states

Our New Kittens

Over spring break[1], our cat had kittens. They were tiny[2], and they made squeaking[3] sounds instead of meows. She licked their faces to keep them clean[4]. They stayed in a basket[5] until they were big[6] enough to jump[7] out. Mom says[8] that we can keep only[9] one. It is hard to decide[10] which one!

1. _____

2. _____

3. _____

4. _____

5. _____

6. _____

7. _____

8. _____

9. _____

10. _____

Draw a picture to go with the story.

Adverbs

> **Adverbs** are words that tell more about verbs. They tell how something happens. Usually, adverbs end with *ly*.

Use the adverbs to finish the sentences.

quickly	sadly	slowly	quietly	too	carefully
easily	fast	loudly	softly	well	gracefully

1. Jenny ran _____ and finished first.

2. Did Sal ride _____?

3. My friend speaks so _____, I can't hear her.

4. Will you work _____?

5. Check your homework _____.

6. Rianne and Bert danced _____.

7. The turtle moved _____ across the yard.

8. We heard Marlene blow her whistle _____.

Adverbs

> **Adverbs** are words that tell more about verbs. They tell how, where, or when something happens.

What does each adverb tell about the verb? Write **how**, **where**, or **when** on each line.

1. Ben walked **near** the beehive. _____

2. Rita whispered **quietly** in my ear. _____

3. Lucy yelled **loudly** at the game. _____

4. Mrs. Holmes exercises **daily**. _____

5. Jared arrived at the movie **early**. _____

6. Adrian's boots are **here**. _____

7. Darla pedaled her bike **quickly**. _____

8. Hannah **often** reads books about animals. _____

9. Drew found the toy **inside** the cereal box. _____

Adverbs

> **Adverbs** are words that tell more about verbs. They tell how, where, or when something happens.

Finish each sentence by adding an adverb that tells how, where, or when.

1. The caterpillar crawled _____.
   how

2. The grasshopper jumped _____.
   where

3. Five ants dragged the crumbs _____.
   when

4. The dragonfly landed _____.
   where

5. The cricket chirped _____.
   how

6. The butterfly flew _____ the flower.
   where

On another sheet of paper, write a story about a garden. Include as many adverbs as you can.

Adjectives

Adjectives are words that describe nouns. Adjectives can tell size or shape.

Example: *Jillian bought the* **square picture** *frame.*

Example: *The* **little** *boy climbed the rope.*

Circle the size and shape adjectives in the sentences.

1. The circular clock is in the hallway.

2. Vinny washed the square window.

3. Carrie bought the thin ribbon.

4. Look at that small sand castle.

5. Yuri has an oval skateboard.

6. Get the dog's long leash.

7. Terrell caught a tiny fish!

8. Hannah found her round glasses.

9. Mae's big bucket is full of sand.

10. That large spider escaped from its cage!

Adjectives

> **Adjectives** are words that describe nouns. Adjectives can tell number, color, size, shape, or anything that adds detail. A sentence can have more than one adjective.
>
> Example: **Four** tulips are in my **colorful** garden.

Circle the adjectives in the sentences. Draw an arrow from each adjective to the noun it describes.

1. Where is the gray bug?

2. Lenny has hot soup and cold milk for lunch.

3. Giant dinosaurs lived many years ago.

4. Eva and Pat used sparkly paint to decorate their pencil boxes.

5. Selma ate a yellow banana and eleven raisins for snack.

6. Jessie is singing a beautiful song.

7. A tired Melina fell asleep on her beach towel.

8. We went to the county zoo on a sunny day.

9. Jacob tried to wash and dry his squirming puppy.

Adjectives

Circle the adjectives.

heavy	walked	old	house	loose	book	shoe
twelve	sneezed	dry	star	broken	sing	whale
silly	hairy	blue	school	strong	parked	wrinkled
gold	wiggle	new	awful	friend	tired	blink

Use the above adjectives to finish the sentences. Or, write your own adjectives on the lines.

1. Whitney held the _____ snake.

2. Jo broke that _____ lamp.

3. Charlie tried to lift the _____ lamb.

4. Bailey rode his _____ scooter.

Write three sentences that contain adjectives. Circle the adjectives. Draw an arrow from each adjective to the noun it describes.

_____

_____

_____

_____

Answer Key

© Carson-Dellosa • CD-104620

Name _____

2.RL.1, 2.RL.7, 2.RL.10

Reading Fiction

Read the story. Then, answer the questions.

Ethan liked to stop by Grandma's house after school. She would fix him a snack. One day, Grandma fell and broke her arm. The doctor said that she needed to rest. Grandma came to stay with Ethan and his mom until she felt better. Now, Ethan fixes Grandma a snack every afternoon.

1. What is a good title for this story?
   a. Helping Grandma
   b. Ethan's Snack
   c. Grandma's Doctor

2. What did Ethan like to do?

   Ethan liked to stop by Grandma's house after school.

3. What happened to Grandma?

   She fell and broke her arm.

4. Where did Grandma stay while she was hurt?

   She stayed with Ethan and his mom.

Name _____

2.RL.1, 2.RL.7, 2.RL.10

Reading Fiction

Read the story. Then, answer the questions.

Our school has a new club. It meets every Tuesday after school. It is not a sports club. It is not a science club. It is a community club! The club members help our town by cleaning up litter. The members read to older people and visit sick neighbors. The mayor came to the first meeting. She is happy the club is helping others. I want to join the club so that I can be helpful.

1. What is a good title for this story?
   a. Cleaning Up Litter
   b. The Mayor's Letter
   c. The Community Club

2. What is another word for community?
   a. neighborhood
   b. sports
   c. science

3. What are three things the club members do?

   a. **clean up litter**

   b. **read to older people**

   c. **visit sick neighbors**

4. Why does the writer want to join the club?

   so that he can be helpful

Name _____

2.RL.1, 2.RL.7, 2.RL.10

Reading Fiction

Read the story. Then, answer the questions.

Jared's mother teaches at his school. Every morning, Jared and his mom ride to school together. One morning, his mom had a cold and could not go to school. Jared called his friend Juan and asked for a ride. Juan lived down the street from Jared. Juan's uncle usually took Juan to school. Juan's uncle was sick too! Jared had an idea. He asked his mom to help him look up the school bus schedule on the Internet. Jared told Juan to meet him at the bus stop in five minutes. They rode to school together on the bus. They decided that riding the bus together was a great plan.

1. What is a good title for this story?
   a. Jared's Good Idea
   b. Get Well, Jared
   c. Jared and Juan Ride the Train

2. Which two people are sick in the story?

   a. **Jared's mom**

   b. **Juan's uncle**

3. What was Jared's idea?

   to take the bus to school

4. Where did Jared find the school bus schedule?

   the Internet

5. What might have happened if Jared and Juan got to the bus stop in ten minutes instead of five minutes?

   Answers will vary.

Name _____

2.RL.1, 2.RL.7, 2.RL.10

Reading Fiction

Read the story. Then, answer the questions.

Heath is a fast runner. He always wins his class race. A new girl came to Heath's class. Her name was Marisa. She was the fastest runner at her old school. Heath wondered if she could run as fast as he could. They had a race after school. Heath and Marisa tied! Now, they are best friends.

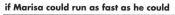

1. What is a good title for this story?
   a. Marisa's Old School
   b. New Friends
   c. First Place

2. What did Heath wonder?

   if Marisa could run as fast as he could

3. What did Heath and Marisa do?

   a. **had a race after school**

   b. **became best friends**

4. What do Heath and Marisa have in common?

   They are both fast runners.

Answer Key

Reading Fiction

Read the story. Then, answer the questions.

My grandpa was a firefighter for a long time. He helped save people from burning houses. Sometimes, he carried people down a ladder. Now, he has a new job. He does not go into burning buildings anymore. Grandpa visits schools to share knowledge about fire safety. He shows students the burn marks on his old jacket. He tells everyone how to stay safe. My grandpa is a hero.

1. What is a good title for this story?
   a. Fire Safety
   b. Grandpa's New Job
   c. An Old Jacket

2. What did Grandpa do at his old job?
   helped save people from burning houses

3. Why does Grandpa visit schools?
   shares knowledge about fire safety

4. What are two things Grandpa does at the schools he visits?
   a. **shows them the burn marks on his old jacket**
   b. **tells everyone how to stay safe**

9

Reading Fiction

Read the story. Then, answer the questions.

Vanessa's brother Luke is in the army. He visits countries that are far away. He helps people who need food or doctors. One day, Luke surprised Vanessa. She did not know he was home for a break. He came to Vanessa's school wearing his uniform. She was happy to see him standing in the doorway of the lunchroom. Everyone said that she was a lucky girl. Vanessa was proud of her brother.

1. What is a good title for this story?
   a. Army Life
   b. Vanessa's Special Treat
   c. Luke's Uniform

2. What are two things that Luke does in the army?
   a. **visits countries that are far away**
   b. **helps people who need food or doctors**

3. Why was Vanessa surprised?
   She did not know Luke was home for a break.

4. What word means the same as *uniform*?
   a. shoes
   b. army
   c. outfit

5. Why did everyone say that Vanessa was a lucky girl?
   Answers will vary but may include she could be
   proud of her brother.

Reading Fiction

Read the story. Then, answer the questions.

Kassie wanted a new puppy. Her mom said that she could get a small one. Kassie picked out a tiny gray puppy named Ruff. Ruff liked to eat. He got bigger and bigger until he was almost as tall as Kassie. Kassie said, "I thought we got a small dog!" Mom smiled and said, "You will have to grow bigger to take care of him!"

1. What is a good title for this story?
   a. Kassie's Tiny Puppy
   b. Ruff Liked to Eat
   c. A Big Surprise

2. What kind of dog did Mom want Kassie to get?
   a small one

3. What happened to Ruff?
   He got bigger and bigger.

4. What did Mom tell Kassie she would need to do at the end of the story?
   grow bigger to take care of Ruff

11

Reading Fiction

Read the story. Then, answer the questions.

I have a funny cat named Sam. He imagines that he is a dog! He likes to run after balls that jingle. He brings them back when I throw them. He chases his tail. He even growls at the mailman! Sam's best friend is my little brother, Robert. He follows Robert around the house and sleeps on his bed. Robert wants to teach Sam to walk on a leash. We are sure he can learn!

1. What is a good title for this story?
   a. Cat or Dog?
   b. Robert's Best Friend
   c. The Mailman

2. What does Sam imagine?
   that he is a dog

3. What are three things Sam likes to do?
   a. **Answers will vary but may include: run after balls, bring**
   b. **them back, chase his tail, growl at mailman, follow**
   c. **Robert around, sleep on Robert's bed.**

4. What does Robert want to teach Sam to do?
   walk on a leash

5. What are some other things you can train a pet to do?
   Answers will vary.

Answer Key

Name _____ 2.RL.1, 2.RL.7, 2.RL.10

Reading Fiction

Read the story. Then, answer the questions.

Brian's little sister Kayce started school this year. They go to the same school. Brian introduced Kayce to his friends at school. His friends thought she was a pleasure to be around. Some of them had little sisters in kindergarten too. They introduced Kayce to their sisters. Kayce was happy to have new friends. She was also happy to have a brother like Brian. She hoped that she could introduce someone to a new friend!

1. What is a good title for this story?
   a. Kayce's Little Friend
   b. New Introductions
   c. Bothering Brian

2. What did Brian do to help Kayce?

   He introduced her to his friends.

3. How did Brian's friends feel about Kayce?

   They thought she was a pleasure to be around.

4. What did Brian and some of his friends have in common?

   They all had little sisters in kindergarten.

5. Why do you think Kayce would like to introduce someone to a new friend?

   Answers will vary.

© Carson-Dellosa • CD-104620   13

Name _____ 2.RL.2, 2.RL.3, 2.RL.10

Reading Fiction

Read the poem. Then, answer the questions.

The Day Emily Sneezed

One very hot day, Emily the Elephant said, "I think I may sneeze."
   So, the grassland animals said, "Excuse us, if you please,"
And ran, oh they did, for they were afraid
   Of what would happen when Emily's sneeze was made.
The giraffes ran for cover and hid behind leaves
   Of the thickest and tallest of all of the African trees.
The warthogs got up from feeding on their knees
   And frightfully asked, "Did Emily say she may sneeze?"
The falcon flew quickly as falcons can do.
   He remembered the last time Emily said, "Achoo!"
The earth had rumbled, and all of the trees shook
   Worse than any disaster you've read about in a book.
So, the animals all covered their ears and closed their eyes.
   But then, they got such a pleasant surprise . . .
Emily the Elephant did not let out a sneeze,
   But instead she laughed and made a cool breeze.
Now, all of the animals went back to their eating,
   And they were happy their land did not take a beating.

1. Where does the poem take place?
   a. in the rain forest   b. in the grasslands
   c. in the desert   d. in the swamp

2. How do you know the giraffes were afraid of Emily's sneeze?

   They ran for cover and hid behind trees.

3. What had caused the earth to rumble?

   Emily the Elephant's last sneeze.

14   © Carson-Dellosa • CD-104620

Name _____ 2.RL.2, 2.RL.3, 2.RL.10

Reading Fiction

Read the story. Then, answer the questions.

Ma Lien

There once lived a poor Chinese boy name Ma Lien. He worked hard in the rice fields, dreaming of the one day he would become a painter. But, Ma Lien did not even have a paintbrush. Instead, he used rocks to scratch on stones or drew pictures with his fingers in the wet sand.

One night as Ma Lien lay in bed, he dreamed that he had a special paintbrush. Whatever he painted with it came to life!

Ma Lien used his special brush to help people. He painted roosters for poor families in his village and toys for children.

A greedy king heard about the special paintbrush. He ordered Ma Lien to paint a mountain of gold for him. Ma Lien painted a gold mountain surrounded by a huge sea. The king ordered him to paint a ship so that the king could sail to the mountain. As the king and his men stepped on the ship, Ma Lien painted stormy clouds that sunk the king's ship.

Ma Lien woke up and went to the rice fields to work. Eventually, he did acquire a paintbrush. Though it wasn't a "special" paintbrush, what Ma Lien painted was special. He remembered the dream and always used his talent wisely.

1. Which of these does not describe Ma Lien?
   a. He lived in China.   b. He was selfish.
   c. He helped people.   d. He wanted to become a painter.

2. How were the king and Ma Lien different?
   Ma Lien used his talent to help people.
   The king was greedy.

3. Who was the most important character in this story?

   Ma Lien

4. What did Ma Lien learn from his dream?

   He learned to use his talent wisely.

© Carson-Dellosa • CD-104620   15

Name _____ 2.RL.2, 2.RL.3, 2.RL.10

Reading Fiction

Read the story. Then, answer the questions.

Paul Bunyan: A Tall Tale

The story of Paul Bunyan begins long ago in the woodlands. When Paul was a baby, he was too big to fit in the house! As he got older, he was so big that his parents had to teach him not to step on houses or farm animals. Back then, people needed lots of trees to build their houses and the railroads. The men who cut down the trees were called loggers. Since Paul was so big, he could swing his ax a few times to cut down a whole forest. He became a great logger.

One winter, Paul was out walking in the snow and found a young blue ox the size of a small mountain. He named the ox Babe. They became close friends. Babe would carry the wood that Paul cut down. He would also take water to the loggers. Paul strapped a huge tub on Babe's back and filled it with water. Sometimes, some would spill out and land in one of Babe's huge hoofprints. That is why there are so many lakes in Minnesota!

Once, Babe tripped and the whole bucket of water spilled. It made the Mississippi River!

No one knows where Paul and Babe are today. Some people believe that they are in Alaska, still cutting down trees. No matter where they are, you can be sure they are leaving their mark!

1. How were Babe and Paul similar? **They are both big and helped loggers.**

2. How does this story say the Mississippi River was made? _____

   Babe spilled a bucket of water.

3. Why did people need lots of trees? _____

   to build houses and railroads

4. How was Paul's job different from Babe's? **Paul cut the trees down and**

   Babe carried the trees.

5. Why was Paul such a great logger? **He could cut down a forest quickly.**

16   © Carson-Dellosa • CD-104620

Answer Key

Name _____

(2.RL.5, 2.RL.10)

Story Elements

Read the story. Then, answer the questions.

The Cat's Bell

There was once a group of mice who had decided to solve the problem of the cat chasing them. Young Mouse said, "Let's put a bell around the cat's neck. Then, we will always hear him coming." The other mice stood and clapped their hands. They put Young Mouse up on their shoulders because they thought it was such a good idea!

Then, Old Mouse stood and asked, "Which one of you will put the bell around the cat's neck?" The other mice looked at one another. They put Young Mouse down and began to think of a new idea.

a.	b.	c.

1. Which picture shows the beginning of the story? a b **ⓒ**

2. Which picture shows the middle of the story? **ⓐ** b c

3. Which picture shows the end of the story? a **ⓑ** c

4. Write four words that could be used to describe the mice.

a. _____ b. _____

c. **Answers will vary.** d. _____

17

Name _____

(2.RL.5, 2.RL.10)

Story Elements

Read the story. Then, answer the questions.

Muffy and the Garden

Ella and her mom worked in the garden. They planted flowers. They pulled out weeds. Muffy is Ella's dog. Muffy watched them work in the garden. It looked like fun to her. At lunch, Ella and her mom went inside to eat sandwiches and fruit. Muffy stayed outside. After lunch, Ella went back outside. The flowers were not in the garden. The dirt was a mess. "Muffy!" yelled Ella. "You were bad!"

1. Who are the characters?

Ella

Ella's mom

Muffy

2. Where does the story happen?

at Ella's house

3. What time of day is it?

noon

4. What is the problem?

Someone dug up the flowers.

_____

5. Who do you think caused the problem?

the dog, Muffy

18

Name _____

(2.RL.5)

Story Elements

We have learned about the characters, setting, problem, and plot of a story. They are called the story's **elements**. Now, let's put it all together!

Follow each step to plan your own story.

1. Plan two characters. Write their names and two words to describe each character. **Answers will vary.**

Character #1 _____ Character #2 _____

a. _____ a. _____

b. _____ b. _____

2. Where will your story take place? Write about your setting.

_____

_____

3. What problem will your characters face?

_____

_____

4. How will they solve it?

_____

_____

19

Name _____

(2.RL.6, 2.RL.10)

Comparing Characters

Stories with more than one important character can be fun to read because the characters are usually different from one another, just as the people you know are different from each other.

Read the story.

City Mouse, Country Mouse

Once upon a time, a city mouse went to visit her friend in the country. The country mouse had spent the day gathering grain and dried pieces of corn in order to greet her friend with a nice meal. The city mouse was surprised to find her poor friend living in a cold tree stump and eating such scraps. So, she invited the country mouse to visit her in the city. The country mouse agreed.

The country mouse could not believe her eyes when she arrived! Her friend lived in a warm hole behind the fireplace of a large home. She was even more surprised to find all of the fine foods that were left behind after a party the night before. The country mouse wished that she could live in the city as well.

Suddenly, the family's cat ran in and chased the two mice away. He nearly caught the country mouse with his sharp claws. As the friends raced back to the mouse hole, the country mouse said, "I'm sorry, friend, but I would rather live a simple life eating corn and grain than live a fancy life in fear!" The country mouse went back home.

The two characters in this story are different from one another. Mark an X in each box to describe the correct mouse.

	City Mouse	Country Mouse
1. She feasted daily on fine foods.	X	
2. She would rather have a simple, safe life.		X
3. She gathered grain and corn.		X
4. She lived in a large house.	X	
5. She was surprised by all of the fine foods.		X
6. She lived in a warm place.	X	

20

Answer Key

2.RL.6, 2.RL.10

Comparing Characters

Read the story. Then, use the details from the story to evaluate the characters.

Last One In Is a Rotten Egg!

"Hurray! We get to swim at summer camp today," shouted Logan as he jumped in the back of the car.

"I don't really want to," answered his brother, Nate. Every summer it was the same. Logan would swim away and have fun while Nate sat on the steps of the pool watching.

The boys spotted their friends right away, and one of them shouted, "Last one in is a rotten egg!" Logan turned to Nate. He saw his brother's eyes fill with tears.

1. What do you think Logan should do? _____

_____ **Answers will vary.**

2. What do you think Nate should do? _____

_____ **Answers will vary.**

Logan called out, "I'm coming!" and jumped in. Nate sat down on the edge of the pool. He watched as the others jumped off the diving board and chased diving rings. Once, a ring landed by Nate, and Logan came after it. Nate stood up and threw the ring back in the water. "That gives me an idea," said Logan. "You can throw in the rings, and we will dive for them."

3. What do you think will happen next? _____

_____ **Answers will vary.**

The boys spent the rest of the afternoon chasing rings as Nate threw them. "Maybe someday, you can throw the rings for me," Nate told Logan as they were leaving the pool.

© Carson-Dellosa • CD-104620   21

2.RL.6, 2.RL.10

Comparing Characters

Read the story. Then, next to each face, write two different ways the story could end, one that is the right decision and one that is the wrong decision.

The Clay Necklace

Miss Jenkin's class spent all afternoon working on projects for Saturday's Native American fair. Lynette and Jeffrey were to make a clay necklace. "I will work on the beads, and you can make the clay sun that will hang in the middle," Lynette told Jeffrey. Lynette carefully shaped beads out of clay and strung them on a piece of yarn. Jeffrey quickly made a ball of clay and smashed it down flat. "I am done," he called and ran outside for recess.

The next day, Lynette was sick and could not come to the fair. Jeffrey's family looked for the necklace he had told them about. There it was. Jeffrey noticed something was different. The clay sun that hung from the middle of the necklace had been carefully carved and painted. It was beautiful!

"There you are, Jeffrey," said Miss Jenkins. "I wanted to tell you how great your work is on the clay sun! You must have spent a lot of time on it."

Right Decision: **Answers will vary.**

_____

Wrong Decision: _____

Right Decision: _____

Wrong Decision: _____

22   © Carson-Dellosa • CD-104620

2.RL.2, 2.RL.7, 2.RL.10

Sequencing

Read the story.

Picnic

My family decided to go on a picnic. I started baking cookies right away. Mom packed bread and meat for sandwiches. Then, Dad put everything in the car. We picked up Grandma.

Read the sentences. Write them in order as they happened in the story.

Mom packed meat and bread.
We picked up Grandma.
We decided to go on a picnic.
Dad packed the car.

1. **We decided to go on a picnic.**

2. **Mom packed meat and bread.**

3. **Dad packed the car.**

4. **We picked up Grandma.**

Draw a line under the best ending for this story.

We all had a good time.

We went to the zoo.

Grandma brought cookies.

© Carson-Dellosa • CD-104620   23

2.RL.2, 2.RL.7, 2.RL.10

Sequencing

Read the story.

Planting a Garden

I help Grandpa plant his summer garden. First, we go to the store to buy seeds. We rake the soil. We dig holes and plant the seeds. Then, we cover the seeds with dirt. We water the seeds so that they will grow.

Read the sentences. Write them in order as they happened in the story.

We water the seeds.
We rake the soil.
We buy the seeds.
We cover the seeds with dirt.
We dig holes and plant the seeds.

1. **We buy the seeds.**

2. **We rake the soil.**

3. **We dig holes and plant the seeds.**

4. **We cover the seeds with dirt.**

5. **We water the seeds.**

Draw a line under the best ending for this story.

Grandpa buys a lot of seeds.

Soon, we will have vegetables to eat!

We buy a new rake.

24   © Carson-Dellosa • CD-104620

© Carson-Dellosa • CD-104620

Answer Key

(2.RL.2, 2.RL.7, 2.RL.10)

Sequencing

Read the story.

Painting My Bedroom

Mom said that I could paint my bedroom. She said that she would help me. We borrowed brushes and bought cans of paint. We changed into old clothes. We rubbed the walls with sandpaper. This made them smooth. We painted the walls green and the trim blue.

Read the sentences. Write them in order as they happened in the story.

We borrowed brushes.
We rubbed the walls with sandpaper.
We painted the walls and trim.
We changed into old clothes.
Mom said that I could paint my room.

1. **Mom said I could paint my room.**

2. **We borrowed brushes.**

3. **We changed into old clothes.**

4. **We rubbed the walls with sandpaper.**

5. **We painted the walls and trim.**

Draw a line under the best ending for this story.

My new room looks great.

I put on my old jeans.

My sister likes the color orange.

(2.RL.7, 2.RL.10)

Character Analysis

> **Characters** are the people, animals, or animated objects that are found in a story. They seem to be brought to life by their actions, and they may even "grow up" or change as people do in real life.

Read the story.

A Real King

Larry the Lion had been king of the grasslands for a very long time, but the animals felt they needed a new king. Larry had become lazy, mean, and selfish. When Larry learned of this, he set the animals free and laughed to himself, "They will beg to have me back!" But, the animals did not beg to have Larry back, and so he moved away.

One lonely day, Larry found a mouse that was balancing on a branch in the river. He helped the mouse to the shore. Later, Larry found a baby zebra who was lost from his mother. Larry was kind and helped the little zebra find his home.

When the animals learned of Larry's kind acts, they asked him to become their king again. They needed a helpful and strong king, which Larry now seemed to be. Larry the Lion had become a real king!

Did you notice that Larry's character changed as the story continued? Complete the lists below by writing three words to describe Larry at the beginning of the story and three words to describe Larry at the end of the story.

Answers will vary but may include:

King Larry at the Beginning
1. lazy
2. selfish
3. mean

King Larry at the End
1. kind
2. helpful
3. strong

(2.RL.7, 2.RL.10)

Character Analysis

Read the story. Then, circle the answers to the questions.

April's Dance Class

April loves ballet class. She goes every Tuesday after school. Class lasts one hour. First, April and the other dancers stretch and warm up at the bar.

Then, April exercises without the bar. She dances in the room with her arms and legs. She is graceful and strong. Dance class is hard work. Her teacher walks around and helps the dancers. He shows Nathan how to hold his head straight. He shows Becky how to relax her shoulders. He teaches them all how to pull in their stomachs.

The next part of class is fun. April loves to jump and do pirouettes. They practice special steps and movements. They move with the music.

April wants to be a ballerina. She works hard. She pays attention to her teacher. She never talks during class. She knows that being a dancer is hard, but April loves it.

1. What does April love to do?

   paint pictures   (dance)   ride her bike

2. Which words describe April?

   fast runner   (hard worker)   colorful

3. What do you think April is like?

   (good listener)   good writer   good babysitter

4. What would April say about ballet class?

   too long   (really fun)   very noisy

5. What does April want to be when she grows up?

   a clown   a dentist   (a ballerina)

(2.RL.7, 2.RL.10)

Character Analysis

Read the story. Then, answer the questions.

Buddy the Cat

Buddy is an old cat, but he still loves to play and explore new things. Once, his curiosity got him into big trouble. Buddy almost died when he was a young cat.

One night after everyone was in bed, Buddy found a spool of thread on the floor. He played with the spool for a while. Then, he started to chew on the thread. Buddy tried to spit it out but couldn't. He kept eating the thread until finally it snapped. After a while, Buddy fell asleep. He didn't feel well in the morning. He lay around looking sad for several days. Finally, we took him to the vet.

The vet removed 26 inches (66cm) of thread from Buddy's stomach. Afterwards, Buddy was very sick and tired, but he was brave. He wanted to live. We visited him every day at the cat hospital. Buddy struggled to his feet to greet us. We knew he was happy to see us.

Buddy survived and is now an old cat. He is still brave and curious. He likes to chase other animals and explore anything that is new, even if it is dangerous. He has had so many close calls that we think he has used up several of his nine lives. We hope he still has several to go.

1. Write four phrases that describe Buddy.

   Answers will vary but may include old, brave, curious, or likes to play.

2. How do the people who take care of Buddy feel about him? How can you tell?

   They love him. They visited Buddy every day. They hope he will live a lot longer. They took him to the vet.

3. What does it mean when we say that cats have nine lives?

   Cats are brave and curious but seem to survive many close calls.

Answer Key

Name_____ 2.RI.1, 2.RI.10

Reading Nonfiction

Read the story. Then, answer the questions.

Teeth

Teeth are important for chewing food, so you need to take care of your teeth. When you are a child, you have baby teeth. These fall out and are replaced by adult teeth. You can expect to have a full set of 32 teeth one day. Brush your teeth twice a day, in the morning and at bedtime. Also, floss to remove the bits of food that get stuck between your teeth. That way, you will have a healthy smile!

1. What is the main idea of this story?
   a. You can have a healthy smile.
   (b) It is important to take care of your teeth.
   c. Adults have more teeth than children.

2. Why should you take care of your teeth?

   so that you can chew food

3. What happens to baby teeth?

   They fall out and are replaced by adult teeth.

4. How many teeth do adults have?

   32

5. How often should you brush your teeth?
   a. only at lunchtime
   b. once a week
   (c) twice a day

© Carson-Dellosa • CD-104620   29

Name_____ 2.RI.1, 2.RI.10

Reading Nonfiction

Read the story. Then, answer the questions.

Healthy Heart and Lungs

Your heart and lungs are important parts of your body. The heart moves blood through the body. Without lungs, you could not breathe. You must exercise to keep your heart and lungs healthy. Your heart starts beating faster when you run fast or jump rope. You may breathe harder too. It is good to make your heart and lungs work harder sometimes. This makes them stronger, and you will also feel healthier. Keeping yourself healthy can be a lifelong practice so that you can have a long life.

1. What is the main idea of this story?
   a. Your heart works harder when you run.
   b. Without lungs, you could not breathe.
   (c) Exercising keeps your heart and lungs healthy.

2. What does the heart do in the body?

   moves blood through the body

3. What do lungs help you do?

   breathe

4. What happens to your heart when you run fast?
   (a) It starts beating faster.
   b. It stops and starts.
   c. It makes you breathe harder.

5. What happens to your lungs when you jump rope?

   You may breathe harder.

6. Why is it good to make your heart work hard sometimes?

   It makes you stronger.

30   © Carson-Dellosa • CD-104620

Name_____ 2.RI.1, 2.RI.10

Reading Nonfiction

Read the story. Then, answer the questions.

The Five Senses

Most people have five senses: sight, hearing, smell, taste, and touch. You see with your eyes. You hear with your ears. You smell with your nose. You taste with your tongue, and you touch with your hands. If you have a cold, your sense of smell might not work right. This makes things taste funny too. You want to protect your senses. Keep sharp objects away from your eyes. Turn down the music before it hurts your ears. Never touch a hot stove with your bare hands.

1. What is the main idea of this story?

   The five senses help you understand the world.

2. What are the five senses?

   sight, hearing, smell, taste, touch

3. What does your tongue help you do?

   taste things

4. What might happen to your senses when you have a cold?

   Things might smell or taste funny.

5. How can you keep your sense of sight safe?

   Keep sharp objects away from your eyes.

6. Why should you not touch a hot stove?

   You might get burned.

© Carson-Dellosa • CD-104620   31

Name_____ 2.RI.1, 2.RI.10

Reading Nonfiction

Read the story. Then, answer the questions.

Helpful Bugs

Some bugs can destroy crops by eating them. Not all bugs are bad, though. Some bugs even help us. Bees move pollen from one flower to the next. This helps flowers make seeds so that there will be more flowers the next year. Bees also produce honey. Ladybugs are another helpful bug. They eat the bugs that chew on our plants. Finally, spiders may look scary, but they are very helpful bugs. They catch flies, crickets, and moths in their webs. If you find a spider inside the house, ask an adult to help you carefully place it outside. Then, it can do its job.

1. What is the main idea of this story?
   a. Bugs can destroy crops.
   b. Ladybugs are beautiful.
   (c) Not all bugs are bad.

2. What do bees produce?
   a. pollen
   b. spiders
   (c) honey

3. How do bees help flowers grow?

   They move pollen from one flower to the next so that flowers

   can produce seeds for the next year.

4. How do ladybugs help us?

   They eat the bugs that chew on our plants.

5. What do spiders catch in their webs?

   flies, crickets, and moths

32   © Carson-Dellosa • CD-104620

Answer Key

Reading Nonfiction
Read the story. Then, answer the questions.

Weather

Weather can be wonderful or very frightening. Rain feels nice on a hot day, but too much rain can cause a flood. People can lose their cars and homes and, sometimes, their lives. A gentle breeze feels good on your skin, but a strong wind can form a tornado, or twister. A tornado can rip the roof off a house. Snow can be fun to play in, but you cannot travel through a snowstorm. If you see a news report that the weather is going to be dangerous, do not be hasty to go outside and watch. It is more fun to watch the weather on TV than to be caught in it!

1. What is the main idea of this story?
   a. You should watch the weather report on the news.
   b. Snow can be fun to play in.
   c. Weather can be wonderful or frightening.

2. What happens when it rains too much?
   There can be a flood.

3. Why is *twister* a good name for a tornado?
   Answers will vary.

4. What can a tornado do to a house?
   rip the roof off

5. What is hard to do in a snowstorm?
   travel

6. What should you do if the news says the weather is going to be dangerous?
   Stay inside and watch the weather on TV.

Reading Nonfiction
Read the story. Then, answer the questions.

The Water Cycle

All water on the earth is part of the same cycle. Water starts out in oceans, lakes, and streams. When the sun heats the water, tiny water drops rise into the air. Water in this form is called steam. As the air cools, the water drops form clouds. When the clouds become too heavy with water, they produce rain, sleet, or snow. The rain falls back to the earth. Some of the water goes into the soil, where it helps the plants grow. Some of the water falls into the ocean. Then, the water cycle begins again. The next time you drink a glass of water, think about where it came from!

1. What is the main idea of this story?
   All water on earth moves through a cycle.

2. Where does the water cycle begin?
   in oceans, lakes, and streams

3. What happens when the sun heats the water up?
   Water drops rise into the air as steam.

4. When do water drops form clouds?
   when the air cools

5. What happens when clouds have too much water?
   They produce rain, sleet, or snow.

6. Where does the rain go after it falls back to the earth?
   Some of the water goes into the soil, and some of it falls back into the ocean.

Reading Nonfiction
Read the story. Then, answer the questions.

Types of Shelter

Shelter is a basic human need. People have always built shelter. The type of shelter a group built depended on their needs, the climate, and the materials that were available. Some groups moved around a lot. The people in these groups needed to have homes that they could take with them. Other people who lived in cold places had to build their shelter from ice and snow. All of the groups' shelters served the same purpose of protecting the people who lived in them.

1. What is the main idea of this story?
   a. Shelter is a basic human need that comes in many forms.
   b. Building shelter out of ice is easy.
   c. Different groups had different purposes for shelter.

2. Which two words mean the same thing?
   a. ice and mud
   b. shelter and house
   c. basic and need

3. Why would different groups' shelters look different from each other?
   the groups' needs, the usual weather of the area, and what they could find to build with

4. Who needed homes they could take with them?
   groups who moved around a lot

5. What purpose does shelter serve?
   protection

Reading Nonfiction
Read the story. Then, answer the questions.

Cities and Towns

Do you know the difference between a city and a town? Usually a city is much larger. In a town, you may have only one school that everyone your age goes to. A city may have many schools for people of the same age. They may have sports teams that play each other for a city title. In a town, you may know most of the other people living there. In a city, you may know only the people on your block or in your building. A city may have more money to provide services, but more people are trying to use those services. There are good and bad things about living in either place.

1. What is the main idea of this story?
   a. Cities are better for young people to live in.
   b. There are good and bad things about life in a town or a city.
   c. People in towns never have any money.

2. How are schools different in cities and towns?
   towns: only one school for people of the same age;
   cities: many schools for people of the same age

3. Who might you know in a town?
   most of the people living there

4. Who might you know in a city?
   only the people on your block or in your building

5. What are some good and bad things about living in a town?
   Answers will vary.

Answer Key

Name _____ 2.RI.1, 2.RI.10

Reading Nonfiction

Read the story. Then, answer the questions.

Building a Community

A community is a group of people who care about each other. A community might include your neighbors, school, sports teams, or clubs. People will often offer to help others in their communities. You can be useful to each other. You might decide to walk your neighbor's dog or go to the store for your grandmother. Your uncle might watch your cat while your family goes on vacation. A family down the street might ask you if you want to go to the movies. It is important for people to feel like part of a community. Always be kind and thoughtful to the people in your community, even if you do not know their names.

1. What is the main idea of this story?

   A community is made up of people who care about each other.

2. What people might a community include?

   your neighbors, school, sports teams, or clubs

3. How might you help someone in your community?

   Answers will vary.

4. How might someone in your community help you?

   Answers will vary.

5. How should you treat people in your community?

   Always be kind and thoughtful.

6. Why do people like to feel they are part of a community?

   Answers will vary.

Name _____ 2.RI.2, 2.RI.10

Main Idea

Read the story. Then, answer the questions.

Visiting Grandma and Grandpa

My family likes to visit my grandma and grandpa. They live far away. When we get there, we hug and hug.

My grandpa likes to play with us. He lets us color in his office. He also likes to make bread. We help Grandpa knead the dough.

My grandma keeps lots of cookies and treats in the house. She has lots of books too. Grandma reads to us all day long.

We love to go swimming at Grandma and Grandpa's beach. We bring our rafts and our towels. We can swim all day. Sometimes, we have a picnic. At night, we have a campfire.

Grandma and Grandpa love it when we visit. They are lonely when we are gone. When we drive home, we talk about what we did. I can't wait until we visit again!

1. What is the main idea of the story?

   The author's family likes to visit Grandma and

   Grandpa's house.

2. What do the kids do with their grandma?

   They eat snacks and read all day long.

3. What do the kids do with their grandpa?

   They play, color in his office, and help him make bread.

Name _____ 2.RI.2, 2.RI.10

Main Idea

Read the story. Then, answer the questions.

Staying Cool

Under the hot African sun, two eyes, two ears, and a nose peek out from a cool river. The huge hippopotamus stays in the water all day long. It is too hot out in the sun! The hippo's large body moves easily in the water. The hippo even sleeps in the cool water.

The sun goes down. The hippo comes out of the water to eat. The hippo walks with the other hippos to a nice, grassy spot. They graze for a couple of hours. Then, they go back to the water again.

1. What is the main idea of this passage?

   Hippos stay in water to stay cool.

2. On what continent do hippos live?

   Africa

3. What is the weather like there?

   very hot

4. How do hippos stay cool?

   They stay in the cool river.

5. Where do hippos spend most of their time?

   in the water

6. What do hippos eat?

   grass

Name _____ 2.RI.2, 2.RI.10

Main Idea

Read the story. Then, answer the questions.

A Beaver Lodge

A beaver lodge is a home built of sticks in the water. Beaver families are busy all day cutting branches and logs with their front teeth. They carry the branches in their mouths as they swim in the stream. Before they build the lodge, the beavers must find a calm place in a stream or lake. Then, they build a dam with logs and branches. The dam stops the fast water and makes a lake.

The beaver lodge looks like a pile of sticks to us. But under the sticks, the beavers have a cozy home. The beavers get inside the lodge by swimming under the water. Their front door is under the lodge. The lodge is a safe place. Beavers can swim quickly into their home when enemies are near.

1. What is the main idea of this passage?

   how beaver families make their home

2. What do beavers do all day?

   cut branches and logs

3. Where is the door for the lodge?

   under the lodge, beneath the water

4. What does the dam do?

   stops the fast water, makes a lake

5. What is the lodge made of?

   logs, branches, and sticks

6. How do the beavers carry branches?

   in their mouths

Answer Key

Name _____ 2.RI.3, 2.RI.10

Following Directions

Read the recipe.

Orange Juice Milk Shake

Ingredients:
2 cups (470 ml) orange juice
1 cup (240 ml) milk
4 tablespoons (60 ml) sugar
1 teaspoon (5 ml) vanilla
10 ice cubes

Directions:
Put all of the ingredients in a blender and blend until frothy. Pour into four glasses and serve right away.

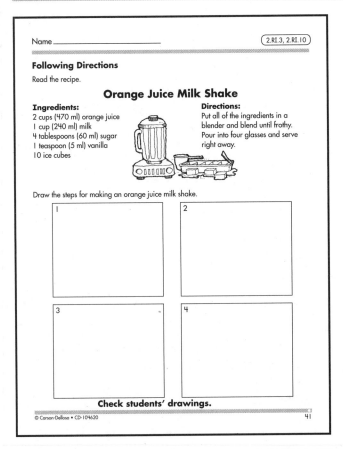

Draw the steps for making an orange juice milk shake.

1	2
3	4

Check students' drawings.

© Carson-Dellosa • CD-104620   41

Name _____ 2.RI.3, 2.RI.10

Following Directions

Read the recipe.

Worms in Dirt

Ingredients:
2 small boxes of instant chocolate pudding
3½ cups (830 ml) milk
1 small tub of whipped topping
10 chocolate sandwich cookies
1 bag of gummy worms
8 clear plastic cups

Directions:
In a large bowl, mix pudding and milk until smooth. Stir in the whipped topping. Put the chocolate cookies in a sealed plastic bag. Crush the cookies by rolling them in the bag with a rolling pin.

Put a little pudding in each cup. Put some cookie crumbs on the pudding. Add a little more pudding and sprinkle the rest of the cookie crumbs over the top. Put two gummy worms in each cup.

Draw the steps for making worms in dirt. **Check students' drawings.**

1	2	3
4	5	6

42   © Carson-Dellosa • CD-104620

Name _____ 2.RI.3, 2.RI.10

Following Directions

Read the story. Then, answer the questions.

Making Bread

The two main ingredients in bread are flour and water. But, there are other important ingredients too. Yeast is very important. Without yeast, a loaf of bread would be flat. A little sugar or honey is needed to feed the yeast so that it will grow and make the bread fluffy. A little salt adds flavor to the bread. Butter or oil makes the bread tender and moist.

After the ingredients are mixed together, the bread dough is kneaded. To knead, you punch, push, fold, and pinch the dough. Kneading may take 15 minutes. The bread must rest in a warm place for an hour or two so that it can rise. Then, you can shape the bread into loaves. Before it bakes, the bread rises again until it is twice as big as when you started.

When bread is baking, the house smells wonderful. It is hard to wait until it is done!

1. What does yeast do to bread?

   makes the bread rise

2. What does salt add to bread?

   flavor

3. How do you knead the dough?

   punch, push, fold, and pinch it

4. What are the ingredients in bread?

   flour, water, yeast, sugar or honey, salt, butter or oil

© Carson-Dellosa • CD-104620   43

Name _____ 2.RI.1, 2.RI.4, 2.RI.10

Vocabulary

Read the story. Then, answer the questions.

Wash Your Hands

You have most likely heard your family and teachers tell you to wash your hands. Be sure to use warm water and soap. Rub your hands together for as long as it takes to sing the ABC's. Then, sing the song again while you rinse them. Soap can help kill the germs, or tiny bugs, that make you sick. If you do not wash your hands, you can pass along an illness to a friend. You could also spread the germs to your eyes or mouth if you touch them before washing your hands. Remember to wash your hands!

1. What is the main idea of this story?
   a. Bugs can make you sick.
   b. Rub your hands together.
   c. You should wash your hands with warm water and soap.

2. How long should you rub your hands together?

   for as long as it takes to sing the ABCs

3. What does soap do?

   helps to kill germs that make you sick

4. What does the word *germs* mean?
   a. kinds of soap
   b. tiny bugs that can make you sick
   c. ways to wash your hands

5. What could happen if you don't wash your hands?

   You could pass along an illness.

44   © Carson-Dellosa • CD-104620

Answer Key

Name _____

2.RI.1, 2.RI.4, 2.RI.10

Vocabulary

Read the story. Then, answer the questions.

The Beach

Have you ever been to the beach? It is fun to play in the sand and then wash off in the water. Tiny fish might tickle your feet when you walk into the ocean. Birds called pelicans fly in circles above the water. When they see a fish move, they dive to catch it. Crabs hurry along the shoreline. You may find seashells in the sand. If you go to a harbor, you will see ships as well as seagulls. The gulls like to eat food that people have thrown away. They are nature's garbage collectors!

1. What is the main idea of this story?
   a. There is a lot to see at the beach.
   b. Crabs hurry along the shoreline.
   c. Seagulls like to eat trash.

2. What can you do at the beach?
   play in the sand and wash off in the water

3. Why do pelicans fly in circles?
   They watch for fish and dive in to catch them.

4. What other animals besides pelicans might you find at the beach?
   crabs and seagulls

5. What does the word *harbor* mean?
   a. nature's garbage collectors
   b. a type of seagull
   c. a place where ships unload their goods

45

Name _____

2.RI.1, 2.RI.4, 2.RI.10

Vocabulary

Read the story. Then, answer the questions.

The Right to Vote

Have you ever voted for class president? Maybe your class has cast votes for the best movie star or type of ice cream. Voting for members of the government is very important. In the United States and Canada, you have to be 18 to vote in one of these elections. Not everyone has been able to vote in the past. In the United States, women were not allowed to vote until 1920. A special law was passed in 1965 to make sure that all adult citizens get to vote. When you vote, you have a say in who serves in the government and what kinds of laws they pass. Some people say that voting is the most important thing that people can do.

1. What is the main idea of this story?
   a. Chocolate ice cream is the best.
   b. Not everyone can vote in the United States.
   c. Voting is an important thing for people to be able to do.

2. Who can vote in the United States and Canada?
   people who are at least 18

3. What happens in an election?
   a. People cast votes.
   b. People have to be 18.
   c. People pass laws.

4. When were US women first allowed to vote?
   1920

5. What happened in the United States after a special law was passed in 1965?
   All adult citizens got to vote.

6. Why is voting important?
   Answers will vary.

46

Name _____

2.RI.5

Text Features

Charts and tables are helpful in organizing information. To read a chart, match the given information from the top and side to find new information in the boxes.

Example: *Who will use the science center on Friday?*

Look at the chart below. Find the science center along the side and follow the row to Friday. You will find Kendra's name in the box.

Centers	Monday	Tuesday	Wednesday	Thursday	Friday
Reading	Sandie	Elena	Sam	Kendra	Evan
Listening	Elena	Sam	Kendra	Evan	Sandie
Math	Sam	Kendra	Evan	Sandie	Elena
Art	Kendra	Evan	Sandie	Elena	Sam
Science	Evan	Sandie	Elena	Sam	Kendra

Use the information from the chart to find the answers.

1. Who will use the art center on Thursday? **Elena**

2. What center will Sam use on Monday? **math**

3. On what day will Evan use the science center? **Monday**

4. What center will Sandie use on Friday? **listening**

5. Who will use the reading center on Wednesday? **Sam**

6. On what day will Elena use the math center? **Friday**

47

Name _____

2.RI.5

Text Features

Read the table of contents. Then, answer the questions.

All about Bears

1. What chapter tells about how bears act in the zoo?
   chapter 9

2. What chapter might tell you how big a baby bear is?
   chapter 7

3. On what page does the chapter on grizzly bears start?
   page 15

4. What chapter will tell you how big brown bears are?
   chapter 3

5. Could you read about bear food on page 38?
   yes

6. On what page does the chapter about bears and people begin?
   page 65

7. Will this book tell you about a teddy bear that lost a button? Why or why not?
   No, the book is about
   real bears.

48

Answer Key

Name

2.RI.5

Text Features

Most chapter books and longer informational books have a **table of contents** page after the title page. This helps you find parts of the book more quickly.

Your teacher has asked you to write a report about animals. In the report, you must answer all of the questions listed below. It would take you a very long time to read the entire book, so you decide to use the table of contents to help you. Write the chapter and page number where you would begin looking to answer each question.

Table of Contents

Animals Around the World

Chapter 1 Mammals (Animals with Fur) 1
Chapter 2 Reptiles (Snakes, Turtles, Alligators)........... 13
Chapter 3 Amphibians (Frogs and Toads) 21
Chapter 4 Fish 35
Chapter 5 Insects and Spiders 49
Chapter 6 Birds.. 57

	Chapter to look in	Page to begin looking
1. How long do lions live?	1	1
2. How fast do sailfish swim?	4	35
3. What do snakes eat?	2	13
4. How long does it take for robin eggs to hatch?	6	57
5. Do spiders bite?	5	49
6. Where do poison dart frogs live?	3	21
7. What do beavers eat?	1	1
8. How long do turtles live?	2	13

© Carson-Dellosa • CD-104620   49

Name

2.RI.6, 2.RI.10

Author's Purpose

Read the story. Then, answer the questions.

Moving

I packed my toys. I put my clothes in a box. My books are coming too. I said good-bye to my room. I said good-bye to my swing set. I said good-bye to my friends. I do not want to go.

My new house is big. I have my own room. I hope my mom remembered my bike. There are kids next door. I wonder if they know how to play hide-and-seek. I am glad to be here.

Draw a picture of the child at the old house and at the new house. Show what the child does at each house.

Old House

Drawings should show details from the story

New House

1. Why did the author write this story? **To compare moving from one house to another.**

2. What do you think is bad about moving? **Answers will vary.**

3. What do you think is good about moving? **Answers will vary.**

50   © Carson-Dellosa • CD-104620

Name

2.RI.6, 2.RI.10

Author's Purpose

Read the story. Then, circle the correct answer to each question.

Charades

Have you ever played charades? Charades is a fun game to play with a large group of friends. All you need to play is a pencil and paper.

Split the group into two teams. Each team writes down book, movie, and song titles on little pieces of paper. The pieces of paper are then put into two bowls. One person takes a piece of paper from the other team's bowl. That person must act out the title. Her team has to guess what the title is.

First, the player shows the team whether it is a movie, song, or book. The player cannot talk or make sounds. Only hand and body motions are allowed. The player shows how many words are in the title. Then, the team watches the player act out the words. They guess and shout out their answers.

Everyone gets a turn. Both teams play. The winner is the team that guesses the most titles.

1. What is the reason this article was written?
   to make you laugh   (to teach you)   to get you to buy something

2. What do you need to play charades?
   a game board   money   (paper and a pencil)

3. How many people can play the game?
   two   three   (a crowd)

4. What do players write on their papers?
   their names   funny stories   (titles)

5. What can't you use when you play charades?
   your pencil   (your voice)   your hands

© Carson-Dellosa • CD-104620   51

Name

2.RI.6, 2.RI.10

Author's Purpose

Read the story. Then, answer the questions.

Bridges

There are different kinds of bridges. Arch bridges are long. Beam bridges are short. Beam bridges may help people drive over rivers or other roads. Arch bridges are very strong. They may help people drive over small lakes or mountain valleys. Other bridges hang from strong wires. They are called suspension bridges and can be even longer than arch bridges.

1. Which bridge is strong?
   arch bridge

2. Where do beam bridges go?
   over roads or rivers

3. Where do arch bridges go?
   over lakes or valleys

4. What are bridges for?
   Bridges help us go over lakes, rivers, mountain valleys, and roads.

5. What kinds of bridges have you seen?
   Answers will vary.

6. What is the author's purpose for writing this passage?
   to inform us about different kinds of bridges

52   © Carson-Dellosa • CD-104620

Answer Key

Name _____

2.RI.7

Reading Graphs

Water or Juice?

The students in Mr. Burr's second-grade class made a graph. Each student put a block on the graph. Look at the finished graph and answer the questions.

Would you rather drink water or juice?

Water ■■■■■

Juice ■■■■■■■■■■■■■■■

1. How many students chose juice? _____**15**_____

2. How many students chose water? _____**6**_____

3. How many more students chose juice than water? _____**9**_____

4. How many students total are in the class? _____**21**_____

5. Does the graph tell what kind of juice the students like? _____**no**_____

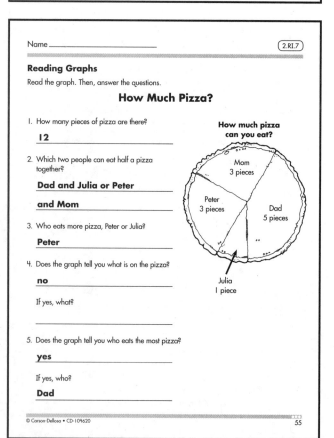

© Carson-Dellosa • CD-104620

53

Name _____

2.RI.7

Reading Graphs

Favorite Frozen Treats

Marjorie asked the kids in her class to name their favorite frozen treats. Then, she made a graph to show the results.

FAVORITE FROZEN TREATS

Number of Kids: 10, 9, 8, 7, 6, 5, 4, 3, 2, 1

Kinds of Treats: fudge bars, frozen juice bars, ice-cream cones, red, white, and blue bars

Read the graph. Then, answer the questions.

1. How many kids like ice-cream cones best? _____**8**_____

2. How many kids like fudge bars best? _____**4**_____

3. How many more kids like frozen juice bars than red, white, and blue bars? _____**1**_____

4. Does the graph tell you how many kids Marjorie asked? _____**yes**_____

   If yes, how many? _____**17**_____

54

© Carson-Dellosa • CD-104620

Name _____

2.RI.7

Reading Graphs

Read the graph. Then, answer the questions.

How Much Pizza?

1. How many pieces of pizza are there?

   12

How much pizza can you eat?

Mom 3 pieces

Peter 3 pieces

Dad 5 pieces

Julia 1 piece

2. Which two people can eat half a pizza together?

   Dad and Julia or Peter

   and Mom

3. Who eats more pizza, Peter or Julia?

   Peter

4. Does the graph tell you what is on the pizza?

   no

   If yes, what?

   _____

5. Does the graph tell you who eats the most pizza?

   yes

   If yes, who?

   Dad

© Carson-Dellosa • CD-104620

55

Name _____

2.RI.9, 2.RI.10

Compare and Contrast

Read the story. Then, answer the questions.

Sisters

My big sister loves to talk. She talks about what she sees and does. She reads books when she is not talking. She talks about what she reads. She reads about people, animals, and places. I like to listen to her. I am quiet. I like to close my eyes and see pictures in my head. I can see the things my sister talks about. I like to draw pictures, too. My sister likes to look at my pictures. She thinks I am smart. I think she is smart.

1. Which sister is more like you? _____**Answers will vary.**_____

2. What do you like to do best? _____**Answers will vary.**_____

Use the details from the story to fill in the Venn diagram.

Answers will vary but may include:

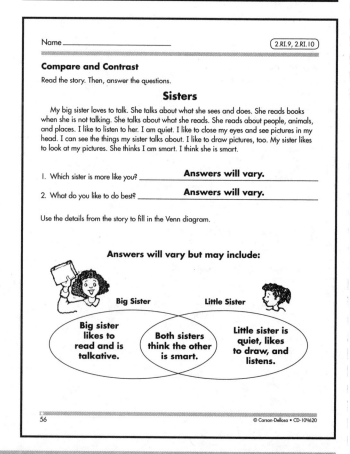

Big Sister — Little Sister

Big sister likes to read and is talkative.

Both sisters think the other is smart.

Little sister is quiet, likes to draw, and listens.

56

© Carson-Dellosa • CD-104620

Answer Key

Name_____   2.RI.9, 2.RI.10

Compare and Contrast

Read the recipes.

Play Dough

Play Dough #1
Ingredients:
1 cup (240 ml) flour
½ cup (120 ml) salt
1 cup (240 ml) water
2 tablespoons (30 ml) cooking oil
2 teaspoons (10 ml) cream of tartar
food coloring

Play Dough #2
Ingredients:
1¾ cups (410 ml) water
2½ cups (590 ml) flour
½ cup (120 ml) salt
2 tablespoons (30 ml) cooking oil
2 tablespoons (30 ml) alum
food coloring

Directions:
Mix the ingredients in a large pot. Cook and stir until a ball forms. Let it cool. Mix the dough with your hands.

Directions:
Boil the water. Mix with the other ingredients in a bowl. Stir until a ball forms. Let it cool. Mix the dough with your hands.

Circle the best answers. Write the other answers on the lines.

1. Which recipe do you think makes more play dough?   #1   (#2)

   Why? **It has more flour and water.**

2. Which play dough needs to be cooked?   (#1)   #2

3. Which ingredient in the second recipe is not in the first recipe?

   (alum)   oil   flour

4. Which ingredients are in both recipes?

   alum   (oil)   (flour)   (salt)

   cream of tartar   (water)   (food coloring)

5. Why don't the recipes tell what color food coloring to use?

   Any color is OK.

© Carson-Dellosa • CD-104620   57

Name_____   2.RI.9, 2.RI.10

Compare and Contrast

Read the story. Then, fill in the Venn diagram.

Alligators and Crocodiles

  Is that a log in the water? It doesn't seem to be moving. But, aren't those eyes? Watch out! It's an alligator! Or, is it a crocodile? Many people confuse alligators and crocodiles. They look and act very much the same.

  Alligators and crocodiles live in the water. They eat fish, turtles, birds, and other animals. Crocodiles have pointed snouts. Alligators have wide, rounded snouts. The upper jaw of the alligator is wider than its lower jaw. When an alligator's mouth is closed, you cannot see many of its teeth. The upper and lower jaws of the crocodile are about the same size. You can see many of its teeth when its mouth is closed. The fourth tooth on the bottom jaw sticks up over the upper lip.

  Crocodiles and alligators are cold-blooded. This means that both animals stay cool in the water and warm up in the sun. Alligators prefer to be in freshwater. Crocodiles are often found in salt water. You may think alligators and crocodiles are slow because they lie so still in the water. But, they can move fast on land with their short legs. Both animals are very fierce. Stay away! They may be quietly watching for YOU!

Answers will vary but may include:

Alligators: rounded snouts, prefer freshwater, and have wider upper jaws than lower jaws

eat fish, live in the water, warm up in the sun, cool off in the water, can move fast and are fierce cold-blooded

Crocodiles: bottom teeth that stick up and have pointed snouts

58   © Carson-Dellosa • CD-104620

Name_____   2.RF.3a

Long and Short Vowels

When two vowels are together, the first one usually makes its long sound, and the second one is usually silent.

Look at these double
vowel words:
road   faint
rōd   fānt

Watch for the vowel *i* to be
followed by the silent *gh*:
night
nīt

Circle the word that names each picture.

1. hear / (hay)	2. (paint) / pant	3. (weed) / wed
4. bet / (beet)	5. (light) / lit	6. fit / (fight)
7. (paid) / pad	8. rough / (right)	9. cot / (coat)
10. (coast) / cost	11. (beads) / beds	12. met / (meat)
13. (goat) / got	14. red / (read)	15. (tray) / train

© Carson-Dellosa • CD-104620   59

Name_____   2.RF.3a

Long and Short Vowels

Look at the words in the list below. Sort the words into two groups, one with long vowel sounds and one with short vowel sounds.

gate	goat	wheat	pack
frog	sock	rug	time
egg	own	gum	man
cue	rate	nest	fine

Long Vowel Sounds
gate
time
goat
own
cue
rate
wheat
fine

Short Vowel Sounds
sock
rug
gum
pack
frog
man
egg
nest

60   © Carson-Dellosa • CD-104620

Answer Key

Name _____ 2.RF.3a

Long and Short Vowels

Look at the words in the list below. Sort the words into two groups, one with long vowel sounds and one with short vowel sounds.

mice	phone	top	blue
ear	mat	face	most
nose	light	fog	nap
pen	long	track	feet
duck	red	sit	cup
fuss	tube	paste	mine

Long Vowel Sounds	Short Vowel Sounds
mice	pen
face	top
ear	duck
paste	fog
nose	fuss
blue	track
phone	mat
most	sit
light	long
feet	nap
tube	red
mine	cup

© Carson-Dellosa • CD-104620

Name _____ 2.RF.3b

R-Controlled Vowels

When a vowel is followed by the letter *r*, it makes a new sound. Say these words to hear the *r*-controlled vowel sounds:

car   bird   fern   church   corn

Circle the word that names each picture.

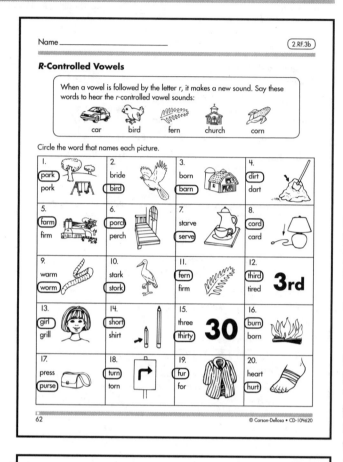

1. (park) pork
2. bride (bird)
3. born (barn)
4. (dirt) dart
5. (farm) firm
6. (porch) perch
7. starve (serve)
8. (cord) card
9. warm (worm)
10. stark (stork)
11. (fern) firm
12. (third) tired **3rd**
13. (girl) grill
14. (short) shirt
15. three (thirty) **30**
16. (burn) born
17. press (purse)
18. (turn) torn
19. (fur) for
20. heart (hurt)

© Carson-Dellosa • CD-104620

Name _____ 2.RF.3b

R-Controlled Vowels

Look at the words in the list below. Sort the words with *ur* or *ar* into the first two groups. Look at the letters of the remaining words and label a third group. Write the words that belong in each group.

burr	artist	feather	return
power	part	shark	dancer
hunger	card	center	furry
turn	purpose	yard	farm
super	surprise	suffer	yarn
start	century	writer	slurp

ur Sound	*ar* Sound	*er* sound
burr	start	power
turn	artist	hunger
purpose	part	super
surprise	card	feather
century	shark	center
return	yard	suffer
furry	farm	writer
slurp	yarn	dancer

© Carson-Dellosa • CD-104620

Name _____ 2.RF.3b

R-Controlled Vowels

Look at the words in the list below. Write the words with *or* in the first group. Look at the letters of the remaining words and label the second and third groups. Write the words that belong in each group.

darkness	storm	during	form
fork	burn	department	born
cartoon	purple	party	nurse
stork	turn	torn	sharp
curl	star	hurry	park
market	worn	doctor	fur

or Sound	*ur* sound	*ar* sound
fork	curl	darkness
stork	burn	cartoon
storm	purple	market
worn	turn	star
torn	during	department
doctor	hurry	party
form	nurse	sharp
born	fur	park

© Carson-Dellosa • CD-104620

© Carson-Dellosa • CD-104620

Answer Key

Reading Poetry

Practice reading the poem aloud with fluency and expression. Then, answer the questions.

Chook, Chook

Chook, chook, chook, chook, chook.
Good morning, Mrs. Hen.
How many chickens have you got?
Madam, I've got ten.
Four of them are yellow,
And four of them are brown,
And two of them are speckled red,
The nicest in the town.
by Anonymous

Check students' drawings.

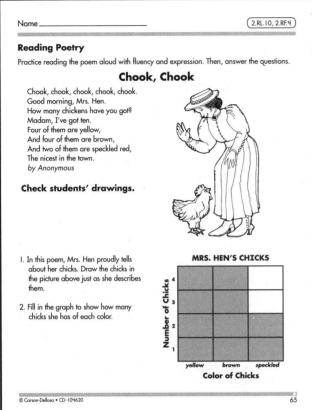

1. In this poem, Mrs. Hen proudly tells about her chicks. Draw the chicks in the picture above just as she describes them.

2. Fill in the graph to show how many chicks she has of each color.

MRS. HEN'S CHICKS

Number of Chicks — Color of Chicks

yellow   brown   speckled

© Carson-Dellosa • CD-104620   65

Reading Poetry

Practice reading the poem aloud with fluency and expression. Have a friend time you for one minute. Record the number of words you read correctly in one minute.

What Animal Is It?

Whisky, frisky,
Hippity hop,
Up he goes,
To the treetop!
Whirly, twirly,
Round and round,
Down he scampers,
To the ground.
Furly, curly,
What a tail!
Tall as a feather,
Broad as a sail.
Where's his supper?
In the shell,
Snappity, crackity,
Out it fell!
by Anonymous

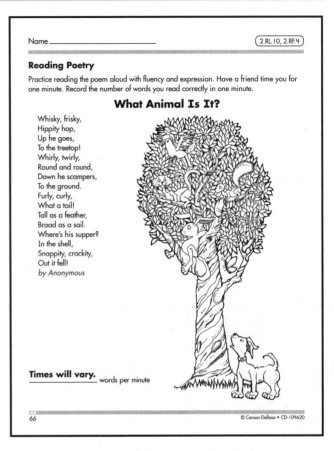

Times will vary. _____ words per minute

66   © Carson-Dellosa • CD-104620

Reading Poetry

Practice reading the poem aloud with fluency and expression. Have a friend time you for one minute. Record the number of words you read correctly in one minute.

Wheels

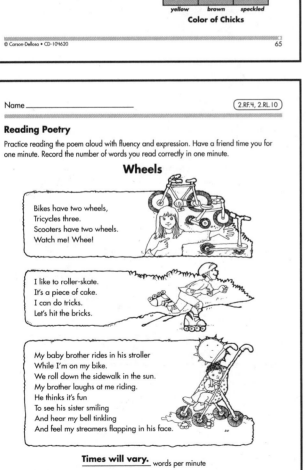

Bikes have two wheels,
Tricycles three.
Scooters have two wheels.
Watch me! Whee!

I like to roller-skate.
It's a piece of cake.
I can do tricks.
Let's hit the bricks.

My baby brother rides in his stroller
While I'm on my bike.
We roll down the sidewalk in the sun.
My brother laughs at me riding.
He thinks it's fun
To see his sister smiling
And hear my bell tinkling
And feel my streamers flapping in his face.

Times will vary. _____ words per minute

© Carson-Dellosa • CD-104620   67

Reading Fluently

Practice reading the passage aloud with fluency and expression. Have a friend time you for one minute. Record the number of words you read correctly in one minute.

Stolen Bike

Adam ran into the house. "Mom, my bike is gone!"
Mom said calmly, "Let's go look for it together."
"Mom, I know I left it right here in the garage last night," said Adam.
Mom and Adam looked in all the places the bike could be. Then, Mom called the police.
A few minutes later, a black and white car drove up. The police officer asked Adam questions about his bike. Adam answered the questions.
The officer said, "You should keep the garage door closed." He told Adam he would call them if he found the bike. The police car drove away.
Mom said, "Let's go shopping at garage sales. Maybe we can find a used bike for you."

Times will vary. _____ words per minute

68   © Carson-Dellosa • CD-104620

Answer Key

Reading Fluently

Practice reading the passage aloud with fluency and expression. Have a friend time you for one minute. Record the number of words you read correctly in one minute.

Playing Outside

Annie and Charlie played outside. The morning sun felt warm on Annie's head. She could smell the flowers that grew next to the house. She picked some ripe strawberries and shared two with Charlie. Annie laughed when Charlie smeared the berries on his cheek and chin.

Charlie played in the sandbox. He pushed the truck in the sand and made a noise with his lips. Later, he pointed at the swing. Annie picked Charlie up and set him in the red swing. She put on his seat belt and gave him a gentle push. Charlie laughed. Annie sat on the swing next to him and counted the 10 red flowers by the house. "When I grow up, I want to take care of plants," said Annie.

"More!" said Charlie. Annie got up and pushed the swing.

"It's almost time for lunch," said Annie. "Mom is making us a picnic. Are you hungry?"

"More!" said Charlie.

Times will vary. words per minute

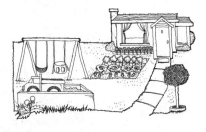

Reading Fluently

Practice reading the passage aloud with fluency and expression. Have a friend time you for one minute. Record the number of words you read correctly in one minute.

Missing Pen Mystery

Mrs. Flores asked her students if they had seen her favorite blue pen with stars on it. Joseph looked at Kyle and whispered, "It sounds like a mystery."

At recess break, Joseph talked to Mrs. Flores. "May we look at the crime scene?" There was a brown spot on the clean desk.

Kyle asked Mrs. Flores if she had eaten any chocolate that day.

"No," sighed Mrs. Flores, "but I wish I had some now."

Joseph looked in the trash can. The boys looked at all of the students' faces as they walked in the door.

After school, the boys went to see Mr. Burk. Mr. Burk loved chocolate. Kyle and Joseph saw Mr. Burk in the hallway. He had a blue pen in his pocket.

"Is that your pen, Mr. Burk?" asked Joseph.

"Well, no," he said as he patted his pocket. "I borrowed it from someone."

"Did you find it on Mrs. Flores's desk?" asked Kyle.

"Yes, I did. I guess I better give it back to her."

"Case closed," said the boys.

Times will vary. words per minute

Reading Fluently

Read the passage aloud. Have a friend time you for one minute. Record the number of words you read correctly in one minute. Practice reading with expression.

Worm Bins

Did you know that worms can eat your garbage? Worms are busy eaters. They eat leftover food, grass, and leaves. Their bodies turn the food into rich soil. You can use that soil to make your garden grow better.

Some people keep worms in a large box. The box is called a worm bin. The worm bin is full of newspaper bits, grass, and leaves. People put their apple peelings, eggshells, and vegetable ends in the worm bin. The worms will eat happily and make soil.

It is not a good idea to put meat in the worm bin. Worms will not eat meat very quickly, and the meat will start to smell bad. Worms cannot eat plastic, foil, or wood. They just eat the food that you usually throw away.

There are two great things about starting a worm bin. You will have less garbage to throw away, and you will have great soil for your garden.

Times will vary. words per minute

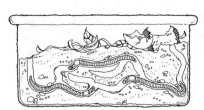

Reading Fluently

Read the passage aloud. Have a friend time you for one minute. Record the number of words you read correctly in one minute. Don't forget to read with expression!

Snowboarding

What sport can make you feel like you are flying? Try snowboarding. It's a little like surfing. It's a little like skateboarding. It's a little like skiing too. To snowboard, you stand on one board and glide down a snowy hill very quickly. A snowboard is shaped kind of like a skateboard, but it is longer and wider. It does not have wheels. It is made of fiberglass, wood, and metal. Snowboards come in many shapes, sizes, and colors. A beginner usually uses a short, wide board.

Snowboarders wear special boots that snap onto the snowboard. Most people ride with their left feet in front. Their toes point in a little. You can turn the board by leaning on your toes or heels. Turning on a snowboard is called edging.

Like any new sport, snowboarding takes lots of practice. Many ski resorts allow people to snowboard on their slopes. But before they do, snowboarders must learn safety tips and rules.

Expert snowboarders can do special tricks. These people are very skilled. They are not beginners. They can ride backwards. They can spin or do a wheelie, an ollie, or a grab. There are many tricks, but some experts just want to go fast down a mountain.

Times will vary. words per minute

Answer Key

Name _____

(2.RL.10, 2.RF.4)

Reading Fluently

Read the passage aloud. Have a friend time you for one minute. Record the number of words you read correctly in one minute. Don't forget to read with expression!

Birthday Fun

Marissa's eighth birthday party was a hit! Her friends said it was the best party ever. Marissa's birthday was in March. It was cold outside. But inside, Marissa's basement was hot. It was a beach party!

Everybody brought a bathing suit and beach towel. The children laid their towels on the floor and put on suntan lotion. At first, they had fun building a sand castle. They used cardboard boxes and sandpaper.

Later, everyone changed into regular clothes and played some games. The first game was pin the leg on the octopus. Each person wore a blindfold and tried to pin a leg onto a picture of an octopus. Ambi pinned the leg closest to the octopus. She won the game.

The next game was a crab race. The children raced in pairs. They had to crawl backwards on their hands and feet. Max was the fastest of all of the kids.

After the games, each guest decorated a pair of sunglasses. They used shells, glitter, feathers, and markers. Everyone looked pretty cool.

At snack time, the kids had hot dogs, blue gelatin dessert with gummy sharks, and lemonade. The cake looked like a beach. It was decorated with a sun, water, and sand. There was shell candy on the sand and a gummy shark in the water.

When it was time to go, everyone got a beach pail full of candy and toys. Too bad they had to put on their warm coats and boots to go back outside!

Times will vary. words per minute

© Carson-Dellosa • CD-104620   73

Name _____

(2.RL.10, 2.RF.4)

Reading Fluently

Read the passage aloud. Have a friend time you for one minute. Record the number of words you read correctly in one minute. Don't forget to read with expression!

Jennifer's Family

Jennifer Hall was adopted by her mom and dad. Jennifer was just a baby when she was adopted. She is eight years old now. She had parents who gave birth to her. Her birth parents loved her, but they had problems. They could not take care of her.

Mr. and Mrs. Hall wanted a family. They wanted to adopt a baby. They went to a social worker who helped them find Jennifer. When she was very little, Jennifer came to live with her mom and dad. Jennifer loved her new family right away. They loved her too.

Jennifer's mom and dad went to a courtroom and said that they wanted to become her parents. They promised to love her and take care of her. The judge signed some papers. Jennifer had a new family. They will be a family forever.

Times will vary. words per minute

74   © Carson-Dellosa • CD-104620

Name _____

(2.RL.10, 2.RF.4)

Reading Fluently

Read the passage aloud. Have a friend time you for one minute. Record the number of words you read correctly in one minute. Don't forget to read with expression!

Lost at Sea

The *Titanic* was a huge ship. It was the biggest ship in the world. The *Titanic* was built to sail across the ocean. The boat had dining rooms, a pool, nine decks, and a gym. The ship was like a moving city.

Many people bought tickets for the *Titanic's* first trip. Everyone was excited. The ship sailed for three days. Then, it hit an iceberg. The ice punched holes in the side of the ship. Water began to fill the hull.

Slowly, the ship sank. There were not enough lifeboats for everyone. Many people got into lifeboats. Other people died in the water. The giant ship broke in half and sank to the bottom of the ocean.

Seventy years later, scientists found the *Titanic*. The ship was rusted and broken. The scientists took many pictures. They did not take anything away from the ship. The scientists put a plaque on the ship. The plaque is in memory of the people who died.

Times will vary. words per minute

© Carson-Dellosa • CD-104620   75

Name _____

(2.RL.10, 2.RF.4)

Reading Fluently

Read the passage aloud. Have a friend time you for one minute. Record the number of words you read correctly in one minute. Don't forget to read with expression!

Return Top

You know what a top is, right? A top is a toy that spins on the floor. Do you know what a "return top" is? You probably do. It's a yo-yo.

To play with a yo-yo, you should first make sure that the string is the right length. When the yo-yo is unwound and near the floor, your hand should be about 3 inches (7 cm) above your waist. If the string is too long, cut it.

Tie a slipknot at the end of the string. A slipknot is a loop that will fit any size finger. Slip the loop around your middle finger at the first joint. Wind the string and hold the yo-yo in your hand. Then, open your hand and toss the yo-yo with a jerk. The yo-yo will unwind and then wind back up. It returns to your hand.

Now, it is time to learn a trick. The basic trick is "the sleeper." Throw the yo-yo a little softer, and it will unwind and stay spinning near the floor. Give it a little jerk. It will come back to you. Try to let it sleep for a count of five. Keep practicing. You have to move your wrist just right.

Yo-yo experts can do many tricks. "Walk the dog" and "around the world" are very popular tricks. The biggest yo-yo ever spun was dropped from a crane. Maybe you can invent a new trick!

Times will vary. words per minute

76   © Carson-Dellosa • CD-104620

Answer Key

Name _____ 2.L.1b

Plural Nouns

A **noun** can be singular (one person, place, or thing) or **plural** (more than one).

Circle the correct noun in each sentence.

1. The three (school, schools) are on the same street.
2. Two (cat, cats) climbed up the tree.
3. The (crab, crabs) has sharp claws.
4. Many (bush, bushes) have berries on them.
5. There are two (Julio, Julios) in my class.
6. That (boy, boys) waved at you.
7. One (doctor, doctors) left for the day.
8. A (tree, trees) can have many leaves on it.

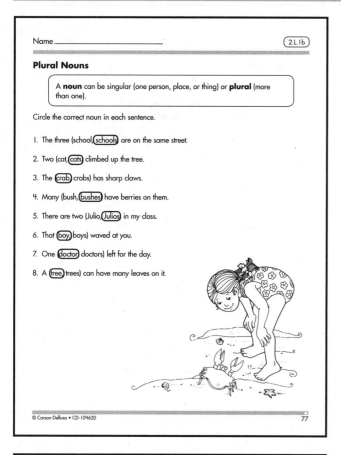

© Carson-Dellosa • CD-104620   77

Name _____ 2.L.1b

Plural Nouns

Use the plural forms of the nouns to fill in the sentences.

Example: penny   cup
*There are six **pennies** in the two **cups**.*

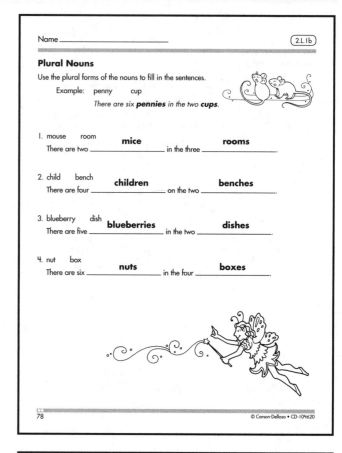

1. mouse   room   **mice**
   There are two _____ in the three   **rooms** _____.

2. child   bench   **children**
   There are four _____ on the two   **benches** _____.

3. blueberry dish   **blueberries**
   There are five _____ in the two   **dishes** _____.

4. nut   box   **nuts**
   There are six _____ in the four   **boxes** _____.

78   © Carson-Dellosa • CD-104620

Name _____ 2.L.1b

Plural Nouns

A noun can be singular or plural. Some nouns become plural by making changes in the middles or at the ends.

Draw lines to match the singular and plural nouns.

goose   children
mouse   people
tooth   feet
child   leaves
foot   women
person   mice
man   geese
woman   halves
leaf   men
half   teeth

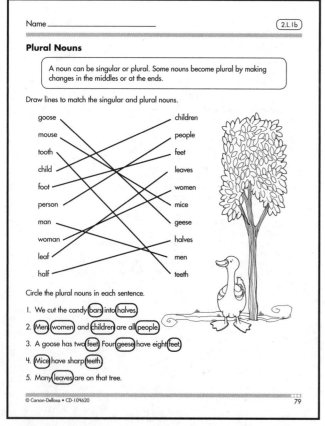

Circle the plural nouns in each sentence.

1. We cut the candy (bars) into (halves).
2. (Men) (women) and (children) are all (people).
3. A goose has two (feet). Four (geese) have eight (feet).
4. (Mice) have sharp (teeth).
5. Many (leaves) are on that tree.

© Carson-Dellosa • CD-104620   79

Name _____ 2.L.1f

Sentences

A **sentence** is a group of words that tells a complete thought. A sentence always starts with an uppercase letter.

Rewrite the sentences. Start each sentence with an uppercase letter. Circle the uppercase letter at the beginning of each sentence.

1. i like studying grammar.
   I like studying grammar.

2. mary will underline nouns with yellow.
   Mary will underline nouns with yellow.

3. sandy and Kit underline verbs with blue.
   Sandy and Kit underline verbs with blue.

4. janice circled the first noun in the sentence.
   Janice circled the first noun in the sentence.

80   © Carson-Dellosa • CD-104620

Answer Key

Sentences

A **sentence** is a group of words that tells a complete thought. A sentence always starts with an uppercase letter.

Circle the first letter of each sentence. Write an uppercase letter above each lowercase letter that needs to be changed.

1. **I** (i)n the afternoon, we learn about science.
2. **I** (i) get to school at 8:45 am.
3. **I** (i) sit down at my desk.
4. **O** (o)livia helps with the calendar.
5. **M** (m)y pencil breaks during math.
6. **M** (m)s. Acker reads a great book.
7. **T** (t)he class eats lunch.
8. **W** (w)e clean out our messy desks.
9. **R** (r)yan picks me up after school.
10. **M** (m)s. Acker will teach us about volcanoes tomorrow.

© Carson-Dellosa • CD-104620   81

Sentences

A **sentence** is a group of words that tells a complete thought. A sentence always starts with an uppercase letter and ends with a punctuation mark.

Add words to make each group of words a complete sentence. Start each sentence with an uppercase letter and end each sentence with the correct punctuation mark.
Answers will vary.

1. runs to
   _____

2. will Dean
   _____

3. get a
   _____

4. the brown cow
   _____

5. begins at noon
   _____

Underline the nouns in each of the sentences.

Check students' work.

82   © Carson-Dellosa • CD-104620

Proper Nouns

Days, months, and holidays are **proper nouns**. A proper noun always starts with an uppercase letter.

Look at the words. Cross out the first letter of each proper noun and write an uppercase letter above it.

1. st. patrick's day   monday   thanksgiving
2. friday   sunday   july
3. new year's day   august   hearts
4. hanukkah   turkey   january
5. saturday   february   christmas
6. october   calendar   november
7. tuesday   leprechaun   december
8. wednesday   valentine's day thursday

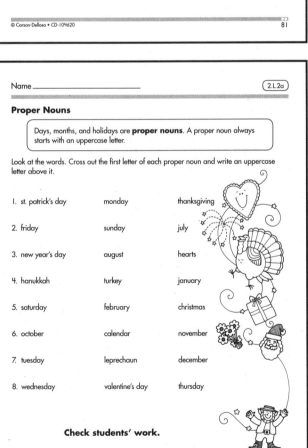

Check students' work.

© Carson-Dellosa • CD-104620   83

Proper Nouns

Days and months are **proper nouns**. Some of these nouns can be abbreviated, or shortened. The complete words and their abbreviations always start with uppercase letters.

Draw lines to match the nouns that name days and months to their abbreviations. (Some months do not have abbreviations.)

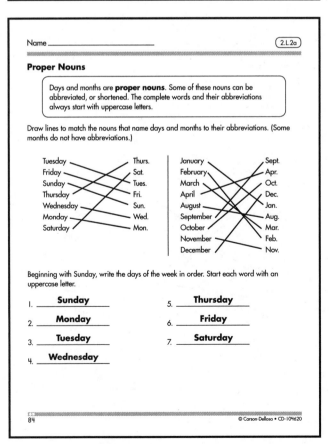

Tuesday   Thurs.
Friday   Sat.
Sunday   Tues.
Thursday   Fri.
Wednesday   Sun.
Monday   Wed.
Saturday   Mon.

January   Sept.
February   Apr.
March   Oct.
April   Dec.
August   Jan.
September   Aug.
October   Mar.
November   Feb.
December   Nov.

Beginning with Sunday, write the days of the week in order. Start each word with an uppercase letter.

1. **Sunday**   5. **Thursday**
2. **Monday**   6. **Friday**
3. **Tuesday**   7. **Saturday**
4. **Wednesday**

84   © Carson-Dellosa • CD-104620

Answer Key

Name _____ 2.L.2a

Proper Nouns

Proper nouns name specific people, places, and things. A proper noun always starts with an uppercase letter. When proper nouns name a city and state, a comma goes between them.

Example: *Orlando, Florida*

Write the names and addresses correctly. Capitalize the proper nouns. Put a comma between each city name and state name.

1. mr. cody stoneson **X**
   461 oak avenue
   littletown ohio 12345

   Mr. Cody Stoneson

   461 Oak Avenue

   Littletown, Ohio 12345

2. dr. coral sargasso **X**
   876 waterway boulevard
   kelp maine 13579

   Dr. Coral Sargasso

   876 Waterway Boulevard

   Kelp, Maine 13579

Draw an X next to each proper noun that names a person.

Name _____ 2.L.2c

Contractions

A **contraction** is two words that are put together to make one word. Some of the letters drop out of the second word when the words are joined. An apostrophe takes the place of the dropped letters.

Example: *did + not = didn't*

Draw lines to match the word pairs with their contractions.

are not	couldn't
were not	isn't
could not	aren't
did not	haven't
do not	wasn't
have not	don't
is not	didn't
was not	weren't

Write a contraction on the line to finish each sentence.

1. We **aren't** going to the circus tonight.
   are not

2. Gerard **didn't** play basketball today.
   did not

3. It **isn't** raining outside now.
   is not

4. You **don't** need a jacket.
   do not

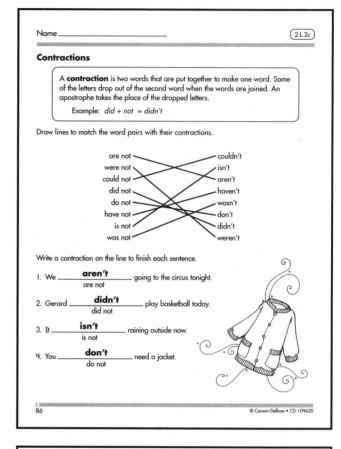

Name _____ 2.L.2c

Contractions

A **contraction** is two words that are put together to make one word. Some of the letters drop out of the second word when the words are joined. An apostrophe takes the place of the dropped letters.

Draw lines to match the word pairs with their contractions.

he is	she's
I would	he'd
she is	they've
you have	I'm
we are	let's
he would	I've
they have	he's
they are	you're
I am	what's
what is	you've
you are	I'd
I have	they're
let us	we're

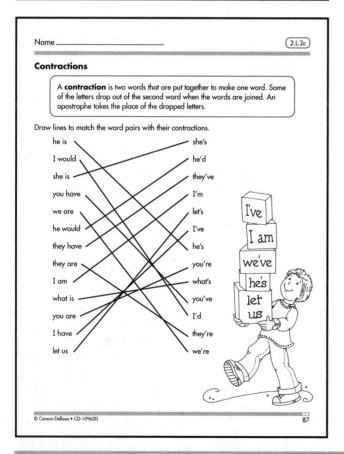

Name _____ 2.L.2c, 2.W.3

Contractions

A **contraction** is two words that are put together to make one word. Some of the letters drop out of the second word when the words are joined. Sometimes the words' letters change to make the contraction. An apostrophe takes the place of the dropped letters.

Write a contraction on the line to finish each sentence.

1. Jill **won't** climb that enormous tree.
   will not

2. The sign says **you'll** need a green ticket to get in.
   you will

3. I think **we're** eating a hot dinner soon.
   we are

4. **What's** the recipe for bread dough?
   What is

5. That **wasn't** the fourth bell.
   was not

6. **She'd** ridden the yellow bus to school.
   She had

7. **Who's** feeding the two hamsters this week?
   Who is

On another sheet of paper, write a story about climbing a tree. Use contractions in your story.

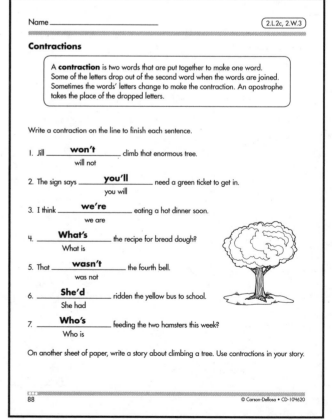

Answer Key

Name _____ 2.L.4d

Compound Words

> Sometimes two words can be put together to make a new word with its own meaning. This new word is called a **compound word**.
> Example: *farm + house = farmhouse*

Write each word pair as a compound word.

1. sun + light = __**sunlight**__

2. birth + day = __**birthday**__

3. every + one = __**everyone**__

4. rain + bow = __**rainbow**__

5. water + melon = __**watermelon**__

6. bare + foot = __**barefoot**__

7. home + work = __**homework**__

8. mid + night = __**midnight**__

9. rail + road = __**railroad**__

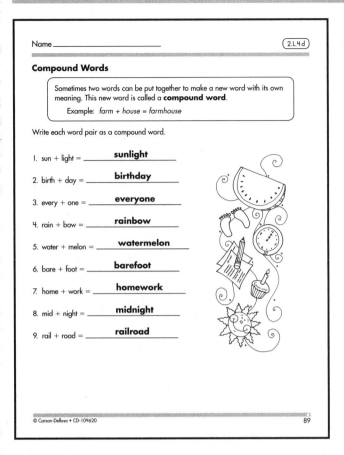

© Carson-Dellosa • CD-104620 89

Name _____ 2.L.4d

Compound Words

> Sometimes two words can be put together to make a new word with its own meaning. This new word is called a **compound word**.

Write each word pair as a compound word.

1. after + noon = __**afternoon**__

2. back + yard = __**backyard**__

3. class + mate = __**classmate**__

4. break + fast = __**breakfast**__

5. flash + light = __**flashlight**__

6. oat + meal = __**oatmeal**__

7. pop + corn = __**popcorn**__

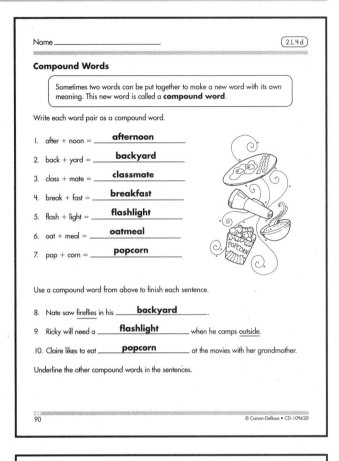

Use a compound word from above to finish each sentence.

8. Nate saw fireflies in his __**backyard**__ .

9. Ricky will need a __**flashlight**__ when he camps <u>outside</u>.

10. Claire likes to eat __**popcorn**__ at the movies with her grandmother.

Underline the other compound words in the sentences.

90 © Carson-Dellosa • CD-104620

Name _____ 2.W.3, 2.L.4d

Compound Words

> Sometimes two words can be put together to make a new word with its own meaning. This new word is called a **compound word**.

Write a compound word on the line to finish each sentence.

1. Amy plays __**basketball**__ at the park.

2. We found a __**seashell**__ on the beach.

3. We saw a beautiful __**rainbow**__ after the storm.

4. Will you come to my __**birthday**__ party on Sunday?

5. Taylor likes to eat __**popcorn**__ at the movies.

6. We camped out in my __**backyard**__ last night.

7. Does your teacher give you __**homework**__ every night?

8. The train travels on a __**railroad**__ track.

9. You should eat a good __**breakfast**__ every morning.

10. __**Everyone**__ had a great time at the pool.

On another sheet of paper, write a story about going to the beach. Include as many compound words as you can.

© Carson-Dellosa • CD-104620 91

Name _____ 2.L.4e

Using a Dictionary

> A dictionary is a book full of words and their meanings. To make it easier to find a particular word, the entire dictionary is written in alphabetical order.

The words below belong in a dictionary. Write each group in alphabetical order.

might	evening	boil
carp	magnet	icicle

1. __**boil**__   4. __**icicle**__

2. __**carp**__   5. __**magnet**__

3. __**evening**__   6. __**might**__

height	pickle	diet
drain	frisky	practice

1. __**diet**__   4. __**height**__

2. __**drain**__   5. __**pickle**__

3. __**frisky**__   6. __**practice**__

92 © Carson-Dellosa • CD-104620

Answer Key

Name _____ 2.L.4e

Using a Dictionary

Use this part of a dictionary to answer the questions.

> **mend** — to heal
> **pastime** — a hobby
> **stalk** — a large stem
> **tragic** — sad
> **wrench** — a tool used to tighten a bolt

1. Where would you find a stalk growing?

   a at the mall   b in a bathroom   c on TV   **d in a cornfield**

2. How do you spell the word that means sad?

   a gratic   **b tragic**   c cragit   d tagric

3. Who would use a wrench?

   a a nurse   b a cook   **c a repair person**   d a baseball player

Use this part of a dictionary to answer the questions.

> stork   petunia   hammer   bushel   candle

4. If these words were found in a dictionary, which would be first?

   a stork   b candle   **c bushel**   d hammer

5. Which word would be last?

   a stork   b candle   c bushel   d hammer

Name _____ 2.L.4e

Using a Dictionary

> A **dictionary** is a book full of words and their meanings. The word you look up is called the **entry word** and its meaning is called a **definition**.

Use the definitions to label each picture with its matching entry word.

> **angle** — shape formed by two lines meeting at a common point
> **parallel** — two lines that never cross
> **perpendicular** — two lines that cross at right angles to make a "+"
> **point** — a dot
> **ray** — a point with a line that goes only one way
> **segment** — two points with a line between them

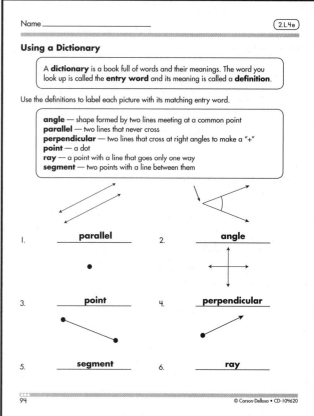

1. _____ **parallel** _____   2. _____ **angle** _____

3. _____ **point** _____   4. _____ **perpendicular** _____

5. _____ **segment** _____   6. _____ **ray** _____

Name _____ 2.L.5b

Synonyms

Read the story below. Decide which word in the box has almost the same meaning as each underlined word in the story. Write your answers on the lines.

> contests   burning   go   enjoy
> unhappy   playground   chilly

Summer

I like summer. My friends and I play games at the park. The sun is hot, but the pool is cool. We are sad when it is time to leave.

1. _____ **enjoy** _____   5. _____ **chilly** _____

2. _____ **contests** _____   6. _____ **unhappy** _____

3. _____ **playground** _____   7. _____ **go** _____

4. _____ **burning** _____

Draw a picture to go with the story.

Name _____ 2.L.5b

Synonyms

Read the story below. Decide which word in the box has almost the same meaning as each underlined word or phrase in the story. Write your answers on the lines.

> takes   each   bright   pals
> neighbor   good   stormy   travel

Going to School

My friends and I go to school in different ways. Trey's mother drives him in her black truck. Jan rides the bus with a girl next door. Tara and Miguel walk to school if the weather is nice. I ride my bicycle every day whether it is rainy or sunny!

1. _____ **pals** _____   5. _____ **good** _____

2. _____ **travel** _____   6. _____ **each** _____

3. _____ **takes** _____   7. _____ **stormy** _____

4. _____ **neighbor** _____   8. _____ **bright** _____

Draw a picture to go with the story.

Answer Key

Name _____ (2.L.5b)

Synonyms

Read the story below. Decide which word in the box has almost the same meaning as each underlined word or phrase in the story. Write your answers on the lines.

pick	large	spotless	box	hop
small	vacation	crying	just	states

Our New Kittens

Over spring break[1], our cat had kittens. They were tiny[2], and they made squeaking[3] sounds instead of meows. She licked their faces to keep them clean[4]. They stayed in a basket[5] until they were big[6] enough to jump[7] out. Mom says[8] that we can keep only[9] one. It is hard to decide[10] which one!

1. __vacation__   6. __large__
2. __small__   7. __hop__
3. __crying__   8. __states__
4. __spotless__   9. __just__
5. __box__   10. __pick__

Draw a picture to go with the story.

© Carson-Dellosa • CD-104620   97

Name _____ (2.L.6)

Adverbs

> **Adverbs** are words that tell more about verbs. They tell how something happens. Usually, adverbs end with *ly*.

Use the adverbs to finish the sentences.

quickly	sadly	slowly	quietly	too	carefully
easily	fast	loudly	softly	well	gracefully

1. Jenny ran _____**quickly**_____ and finished first.

2. Did Sal ride _____**well**_____ ?

3. My friend speaks so _____**quietly**_____, I can't hear her.

4. Will you work _____**too**_____ ?

5. Check your homework _____**carefully**_____.

6. Rianne and Bert danced _____**gracefully**_____.

7. The turtle moved _____**slowly**_____ across the yard.

8. We heard Marlene blow her whistle _____**loudly**_____.

98   © Carson-Dellosa • CD-104620

Name _____ (2.L.6)

Adverbs

> **Adverbs** are words that tell more about verbs. They tell how, where, or when something happens.

What does each adverb tell about the verb? Write **how**, **where**, or **when** on each line.

1. Ben walked **near** the beehive. _____**where**_____

2. Rita whispered **quietly** in my ear. _____**how**_____

3. Lucy yelled **loudly** at the game. _____**how**_____

4. Mrs. Holmes exercises **daily**. _____**when**_____

5. Jared arrived at the movie **early**. _____**when**_____

6. Adrian's boots are **here**. _____**where**_____

7. Darla pedaled her bike **quickly**. _____**how**_____

8. Hannah **often** reads books about animals. _____**when**_____

9. Drew found the toy **inside** the cereal box. _____**where**_____

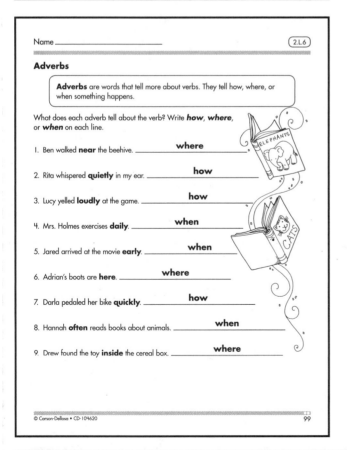

© Carson-Dellosa • CD-104620   99

Name _____ (2.W.3, 2.L.6)

Adverbs

> **Adverbs** are words that tell more about verbs. They tell how, where, or when something happens.

Finish each sentence by adding an adverb that tells how, where, or when.

Answers will vary.

1. The caterpillar crawled _____
    how

2. The grasshopper jumped _____
    where

3. Five ants dragged the crumbs _____
    when

4. The dragonfly landed _____
    where

5. The cricket chirped _____
    how

6. The butterfly flew _____ the flower.
    where

On another sheet of paper, write a story about a garden. Include as many adverbs as you can.

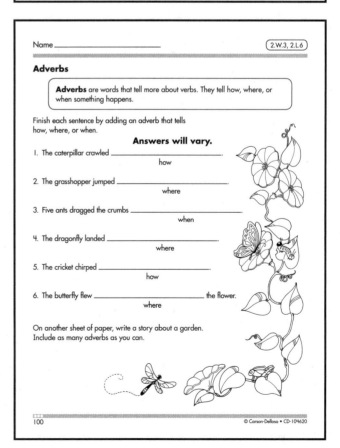

100   © Carson-Dellosa • CD-104620

© Carson-Dellosa • CD-104620

Answer Key

Adjectives

Adjectives are words that describe nouns. Adjectives can tell size or shape.

Example: *Jillian bought the **square picture** frame.*

Example: *The **little** boy climbed the rope.*

Circle the size and shape adjectives in the sentences.

1. The (circular) clock is in the hallway.
2. Vinny washed the (square) window.
3. Carrie bought the (thin) ribbon.
4. Look at that (small) sand castle.
5. Yuri has an (oval) skateboard.
6. Get the dog's (long) leash.
7. Terrell caught a (tiny) fish!
8. Hannah found her (round) glasses.
9. Mae's (big) bucket is full of sand.
10. That (large) spider escaped from its cage!

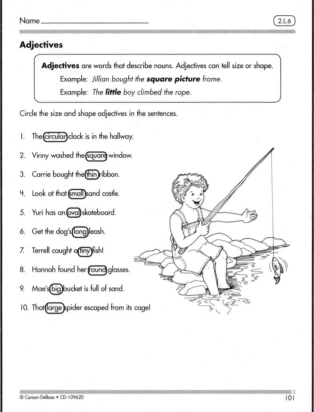

Adjectives

Adjectives are words that describe nouns. Adjectives can tell number, color, size, shape, or anything that adds detail. A sentence can have more than one adjective.

Example: ***Four** tulips are in my **colorful** garden.*

Circle the adjectives in the sentences. Draw an arrow from each adjective to the noun it describes.

Check students' arrows.

1. Where is the (gray) bug?
2. Lenny has (hot) soup and (cold) milk for lunch.
3. (Giant) dinosaurs lived (many) years ago.
4. Eva and Pat used (sparkly) paint to decorate their (pencil) boxes.
5. Selma ate a (yellow) banana and (eleven) raisins for snack.
6. Jessie is singing a (beautiful) song.
7. A (tired) Melina fell asleep on her (beach) towel.
8. We went to the (county) zoo on a (sunny) day.
9. Jacob tried to wash and dry his (squirming) puppy.

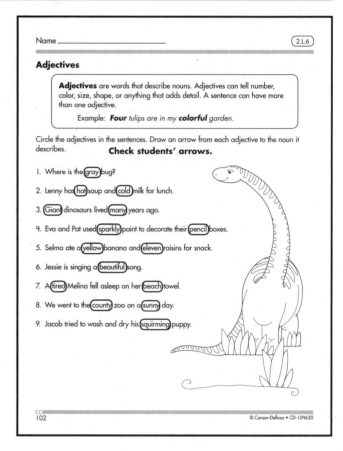

Adjectives

Circle the adjectives.

(heavy)	walked	(old)	house	(loose)	book	shoe
(twelve)	sneezed	(dry)	star	(broken)	sing	whale
(silly)	(hairy)	(blue)	school	(strong)	parked	(wrinkled)
(gold)	wiggle	(new)	(awful)	friend	(tired)	blink

Use the above adjectives to finish the sentences. Or, write your own adjectives on the lines.

Answers will vary.

1. Whitney held the _____ snake.
2. Jo broke that _____ lamp.
3. Charlie tried to lift the _____ lamb.
4. Bailey rode his _____ scooter.

Write three sentences that contain adjectives. Circle the adjectives. Draw an arrow from each adjective to the noun it describes.

Check students' work.

_____

_____

_____

_____

_____

Congratulations!

receives this award for

Signed

Date

actor	apply	aquarium	artist
banana	bicycle	blaze	blouse
borrow	branch	bubble	business
cactus	carrot	chat	clerk

© CD

coast	**crowd**	**daydream**	**desk**
doorway	**drill**	**dust**	**govern**
either	**enjoy**	**expect**	**famous**
feather	**flash**	**flight**	**forgive**

© CD

grand	giant
hasty	harbor
imagine	hungry
knight	journal

fruit	friendship
hammer	grape
hound	history
jingle	island

© CD

mask

nail

pleasure

prowl

liberty

mountain

only

proud

ladder

middle

neighbor

pretend

knowledge

measure

narrow

powerful

quart	railroad	rainwater	remove
respect	result	season	share
skill	smooth	snack	special
speech	spend	spray	squeak

© CD

thirsty

© CD

umbrella

© CD

wagon

© CD

younger

© CD

thick

trash

vegetable

yank

© CD

© CD

© CD

© CD

talent

thread

vacation

woodpecker

© CD

© CD

© CD

© CD

stomach

thoughtful

useful

wheat

© CD

© CD

© CD

© CD